# WINNING POKER FOR THE SERIOUS PLAYER

***About Edwin Silberstang***

"The man many consider the greatest gambling authority in the world."

Len Miller, Editor-in-Chief, Gambling Times Magazine.

"Ed Silberstang knows more about gambling from the inside and the outside than anyone writing on the subject today."

John Luckman, Gambler's Book Club.

*To Ben Lipson*

## ABOUT THE AUTHOR

Edwin Silberstang is acknowledged by the top professionals in the gambling world as the leading authority on games in America. His first book, Playboy's Book of Games, published in 1972, was an instant best seller and a selection of the Book of the Month Club.

Since then, Silberstang has published over thirty books dealing with games, gambling and the Vegas scene. His expertise has been used in the entertainment world, and he was the technical adviser on the film, Big Town, a story about a young gambler starring Matt Dillon, produced by Columbia Pictures.

In addition, he has written and starred in his own videos about gambling, and has appeared on many television and radio shows throughout the country. He is constantly called upon as a consultant and teacher as well.

Silberstang's success in the field of gambling writing comes from a skill as a novelist combined with a vast knowledge of gambling. His writing is clear and concise and he not only is able to present information but to make it interesting and fascinating.

Now he brings his expertise to high level poker, a field he has mastered, where his solid knowledge of the game has been acknowledged by world champions and other legendary figures of the game.

# WINNING POKER FOR THE SERIOUS PLAYER

Edwin Silberstang

- Gambling Research Institute -
## Cardoza Publishing

**Cardoza Publishing**, publisher of **Gambling Research Institute** (GRI) books, is the foremost gaming publisher in the world with a library of more than 50 up-to-date and easy-to-read books and strategies.

These authoritative works are written by the top experts in their fields and with more than 3,500,000 books in print, represent the best-selling and most popular gaming books anywhere.

**Printing History**

| First Printing | August 1992 |
| Second Printing | March 1994 |

Library of Congress Catalog Card No: 92-72608
ISBN: 0-940685-32-9
Front Cover Photo by Ron Charles
Author Photo by Carole Donovan

**CARDOZA PUBLISHING**

P.O. Box 1500, Cooper Station, New York, NY 10276 • (718)743-5229

**Write for your free catalogue of gambling books, advanced strategies, and computer items.**

# Table of Contents

## XI. Other Poker Games 189

## XII. A Final Winning Word 212

## Glossary 217

# I. INTRODUCTION

Poker is a game that combines the elements of skill, luck and psychology in a fascinating way. No single element stands alone, and together they make this the most interesting of all card games. And even better, it is a game always played for money.

In this book, we're going to analyze all these elements and show how to combine them to your advantage. The most important is skill, and once you know how to really play poker, you're going to find yourself a winner. The cards you get are secondary, it's what you do with the cards you're dealt that will determine whether or not you make money at poker.

We're going to analyze various hands in all the popular poker games, and many variations of those games, so that, whether you play at home, in a club or casino, you'll be at the top of your form. You'll know what you are doing, while the others will trust to luck.

If we combine the skill you'll learn with psychology, which is the art of deception in poker, as well as the ability to read other players' hands by their gestures and bets, you'll be using the poker table as you would a bank, where you'll be making regular withdrawals of other players' money.

By the time you finish this book, you'll be comfortable in any poker game, and you'll be a winner in all the games you decide to play. We'll show you how to master the strategies necessary to be a great poker player and how to handle yourself at the table. We'll make your table image one that will cause other players to fear you and be intimidated by your play. We'll show you when to be aggressive and when to slow down, when to bet big and when to not play hands.

What we're presenting in this book is a complete course in winning poker, and the end result will be a fatter bankroll for you, plus a lot of fun as well. By the time you finish this book you'll have a whole new approach to this most fascinating of games, one that will make you a big winner!

# II. THE FIVE FUNDAMENTAL PRINCIPLES OF WINNING POKER

Many players who have gambled at poker for years have lost track of the fundamental winning principles of poker. When any of these principles are violated, a losing situation presents itself.

Therefore, we must study once more the five fundamental principles which assure victory at the poker table.

**1. The only purpose in playing poker is to win money.**

This is very important. Unless you're playing penny-ante poker with your mother and maiden aunts, you're there to make money. The final count of chips and/or cash determines who has won and who has lost. The losers have less money and the winners more money. Simple as that, but arriving at that goal of winning takes many factors, all of which will be covered.

When you sit down for a serious game of poker, don't think in terms of how much you're going to lose. Think of winning, and turn your head around so that winning is the most important consideration in the game. If you do this, you're on your way to becoming a winner. There are many other pastimes for fun and recreation. Serious poker is not one of them, although winning is a wonderful thing.

**2. Be alert at all times.**

In the movies, the tough poker player can afford to swig from a bottle of gin, or pour himself endless belts or shots of rye. After all, he's playing from a script, and if the script tells him that he's a winner, then he'll be a winner. Nothing like that is foreordained in real life. There is no script everyone is following, and therefore, the player must be at the top of his form all during his session of serious poker.

In order to do this, he or she must not feel tired or weakened by a cold or illness. If that's the case, forego the poker game, and curl up with a good book and some hot tea or chicken soup in your bed. But don't be playing poker with the sniffles or a blinding headache. Don't play if you're worn out or tired. You must be both physically and mentally alert at the table. Otherwise, pass up the game.

Don't drink while playing and don't go to the table with even one drink under your belt. Alcohol impairs judgment, and even worse, it makes cowards into brave men, gets them up till the reality hits them, and the depression begins. Sometimes a drunk goes crazy at a game and runs over all the other players with an incredible run of great cards.

But more often, the drunk is the loser, the sucker, the chump at the table. I've been at games where there is one roaring drunk in on every hand, betting and raising the limit. Do you know what happens? Suddenly the whole character of the game changes. We may be seven strangers facing the drunk, but an unwritten code emerges; everyone goes after the drunk.

Sometimes this strategy backfires, for players will stay in with weaker cards, knowing no matter how weak their cards are, the drunk's will probably be weaker. Then that player will lose out to another player in with stronger hands, or will lose to the drunk, who will draw a high pair or some card to beat the player's weak cards.

The important thing to remember is this; don't you be the drunk or the chump. Stay away from drinking. If everyone else at the table is drinking, fine and dandy. That makes your chances of winning even stronger. You'll be playing with a clear mind while the opponents will have their judgment impaired.

**3. Play only in games you can afford to play in, either financially or emotionally.**

I personally know a millionaire who can't play beyond a certain fixed limit, whereas he can afford financially to play at five times that limit with his money. The reason he doesn't play at bigger games is because he can't afford to emotionally. His heart starts racing during playable hands; a loss devastates him, he appears to be a motorcycle at the table with the engine revved up to max torque, but the cycle isn't moving. He knows this about himself, and he sticks to lower level games.

On the other hand, I know a few guys in Vegas who call themselves pros who are always at games they can't afford to be at - financially. If they take a big loss, they're devastated financially, as well as emotionally, and it may take a few weeks for them to lick their wounds and raise some money to get back in action.

Then they go and play in too big a game, and hope for a run of good cards to get a monster win, but usually the result is the opposite. They're playing with **scared money**, money they can't afford to lose because they're under-capitalized at the table. They play more cautiously and don't raise when they should to drive other players out. In other words, as we shall see in the various theorems of winning poker, they're playing like the chumps, the losers.

Other players smell out scared money players, and they're hit with checks from all sides of the table. I'm going to use the words *checks* and *chips* interchangeably in this book, to denote units representing cash that most poker players use rather than real cash.

Anyway, the scared player is raised and reraised when he has any kind of playable hand, till his head is spinning and his hands are shaking. He stands no chance against perceptive and intelligent and aggressive players.

**4. Have sufficient capital for the game you're playing.**

This is a corollary of the above principle. Most games in casinos require a minimum buy-in, but this amount is not sufficient for

12

real play.

For example, in the $5-10 poker games on the Las Vegas Strip, the minimum buy-in is $50, which means that the prospective poker player, when he sits down, must have $50 in front of him, ready for play. After the sit down, the minimum buy-in rule is waived. Thus, a player who started with $50, may be down to $10 after losing a hand, but he can play with the $10 and doesn't have to buy more checks to stay in action.

He not only has scared money now but he has no chance of making any money, because after his $10 is used up, he's going to have to sit and watch the action in the game. He'll be "all in" and not able to make any future bets, and only a portion of the pot will belong to him if he wins.

If there's one thing I've seen over and over again in my years of poker playing, it's foolish players who are all in just when they get a monster hand. I watched a pot build to $1,500 once, and the winning hand was four 8s, held by a player who was all in, and could only bet $20. His share of that pot was about $100, while Aces up took the other $1,400.

**Bankrolling Rules of Thumb**

What capital do you need for a game? It depends on the stakes, the type of game you're in, and the ante structure.

In a game of $5-10 or $10-20 seven-card stud poker, with a medium ante (10% of the minimum bet) you'll need forty times the minimum bet to stay in action for a while.

Thus in the $5-10 game, you'd need $200, and in the higher game, $400. That's a reasonable stake. And since many of the casino games are **table stake** games, which means that you can't put more money into play on the table during the playing of a hand, it's always advisable to have at least 20 times the minimum bet on the table at all times.

This will allow you to get in good action if you have a strong hand, and won't leave you in the cold, moaning "all in" while you watch the weaker hands carve up the pot.

In a bigger game, such as $100-$200, where the ante is large (25% of the minimum bet), you're going to need at least 50 times the minimum bet as a minimum stake. Also never leave yourself with less than 25 times the minimum bet on the table.

In a game like Hold 'em, which has much more action than Seven-Card Stud, the minimum stake you should have is 100 times the minimum bet. For example, in even such a paltry Hold 'em game like $2-$4, you should have $200 on the table in front of you. In a $5-$10 Hold 'em game, you'd need $500.

There is more action in Hold 'em, more raising and more bluffing, and the ante is usually bigger. For example, in a $2-$4 game, the ante is 50¢ in the California poker clubs, which is a hefty 25% of the minimum bet.

To repeat the two essential rules here; have sufficient capital for your game, and in casino games where you're limited to table stakes, keep enough money on the table to be able to bet fully in any round of poker, including raises and reraises.

## 5. Know when to leave the table.

This is extremely important. If you're going to play poker either professionally or as a way to make money, then you can't look at poker as individual sessions of play, but as one long poker game, that's going on indefinitely. You step into it and step out of it. It doesn't matter if you made $250 today, if you've lost $6,000 a week before. You're not a $250 winner; you're a $5,750 loser. You should keep a running count of your wins and losses. It doesn't matter if you win more than you lose in terms of poker sessions, or vice-versa.

What is important is how you stand at the end of your last play. Are you ahead or behind? If you're ahead, you're a winner; if you're behind, you're losing, and nothing you can think about or rationalize about is going to change this.

## Minimizing Losses

The most important thing is to know just what you can afford

14

to lose in one session of play. I play by certain principles. I will bring, for example, my $400 to a $10-$20 game, and if I lose that, invest another $200 in the game, or 60 times the minimum bet. I'll only do this if the game is a good one, where I feel I'm better than most of the players and there are a couple of outright suckers in the game.

If I feel uncomfortable in the game, feel unlucky or whatever vibes I feel that aren't good, I'll probably be out of the game with a $200 loss at the outset. There's always another game and another day.

That is my limit, 60 times the minimum bet. Now, I know a number of pros, and some of them do very well and others not so well. The main difference between them is often that the ones doing badly have stubbornly stayed in a game that they should have been out of a long time before.

In a $30-$60 game I know a player who dropped $6,000 in a horrendous ten-hour session that left him drained, with stomach pains and a blinding headache that lasted two days. At the worst, he should have dropped $1,800 in that game. At the worst. $1,800 can be made up in one session of play. $6,000 cannot unless miracle cards are flying out of the sky, and you're beating players with monster hands.

That $6,000 loss forced the pro to stop playing for three weeks, during which time he didn't have the possibility of any other income. When he came back to play, he couldn't shake the thought of that loss, and when he booked small wins, they didn't mean anything to him. He won $600, $800 and $500 in three sessions after returning, giving him $1,900 in profits.

He would have been up by $100 if he had played sanely and lost only $1,800. Instead he was still behind by $4,100, so he went up to a $50-$100 game, and got destroyed trying to win back the losses. He was doing everything wrong; in poker parlance, he was **on tilt**, off-balance, making wrong moves.

If you're playing Hold 'Em, then 100 times the minimum bet should be the maximum loss. That can be made up. 150 times the minimum bet is too rich, and is extremely difficult to make up in one session of play. In fact, if you start with $500 in a $5-$10 Hold' em game, don't test the 100 times losses, just get out when you're down to $100 rather then have to put more money on the table after a big losing hand.

Cheap losses can be made up. Small losses don't destroy you. A monster loss kills you financially and psychologically. Avoid them. Play sanely and keep your losses at a sane level, so you can make them up the next game or in a couple of sessions of poker.

**Maximizing Wins**

Well, that's all bad news we were discussing up above. How about some good news? We find ourselves ahead. When do we leave? That's a tough question. If you're ahead, the first thing you want to think about is leaving a winner. That is, if you're winning enough money.

If you're ahead $55 in a $15-$30 game, the winnings are so inconsequential that they don't count. You can lose that before Fourth Street, plus some of your original bankroll.

The decision to leave, therefore, occurs when you're ahead a substantial amount. Do you stay in and try to win more? Do you put aside some of the winnings and when you get down to that, do you leave? Just when do you quit the game?

There is no one answer to the question. The player must ask himself or herself several questions. First of all, is it a good game? Is it a game in which you are the top player, or among the top, with several weakies in the game? If it's a good game, then you want to play as long as possible. Just as you want to avoid the single killing monster loss, if possible, you want that big monster win, which will carry you past a host of small losses.

**When to Quit**

Other considerations enter into the picture. Suppose it's a great game and you're rolling over the table, but you're getting tired, and have already made a couple of bad plays in the last half-hour.

It's time to either get up from the game, or take a break to refresh yourself. If you're playing in a casino, stroll to the coffee shop and get something to eat. If you're not hungry, or can't eat while playing, then some coffee or tea would be good. Don't read anything; rest your eyes and brain and just sit there and relax in the coffee shop.

If you find a half hour of this will refresh you, then go back into the game. If you're still tired, gather up your checks and leave the table. Your playing is over for that one session.

Various pros and top-level players use different criteria to decide when to leave. Some I know treat it strictly as a business and put in so many hours at a time, with the outer limit being eight. However, a couple of these players will stay beyond the eight-hour limit if the game is good and they're winning steadily.

Others will only stay in a good game, where there are some weak players they know they can outplay. If these players leave, if the table in Vegas is just filled with "locals," they're gone also. A number will want a win, and will stay if their losses are moderate, till they are ahead, no matter how long it takes. This I don't recommend.

Remember the concept of the one long poker game you're playing, no matter how many games you play. If you have a moderate loss, and you're tired, leave. You can easily make it up.

Sometimes the game is bad, with tough players, but you're getting miraculous cards and winning pot after pot, outdrawing everyone at the table. Ride the streak. Stay with the rush. But when it deserts you, when you've lost two hands in a row, leave the table.

You might want to try money management with a stop-loss strategy. If you're winning at least 30 times the minimum bet, make a mental note to leave the table when you're ahead only 20 times the minimum bet, so you can leave a winner.

Suppose you've been playing in a $15-$30 game for close to four hours and after a rollercoaster ride, against players who don't make this a particularly good game, you find yourself ahead $450.

17

You're getting a little tired but still can make alert moves. Make a mental note that if you lose a hand or two and only have $300, you leave the table. That's much better than playing till you lose everything you won.

Note that I considered the time element. If you sit down and after 45 minutes are winning $450, and find the game good, there's no point in leaving when you're ahead $300. You want to have the possibility of winning much more. Poker is not a game for cautious people.

Those are the parameters I would feel comfortable with in leaving a winner.

One final note: If you've been losing all session, and finally take a couple of hands that bring you back to even, and it's already been a long night, pack it in right then and there. There's nothing worse, psychologically speaking, than to finally break even, and then watch it all drain away one more time. If the game is a struggle, get out. That's not the ideal game for you.

# III. OVERALL WINNING STRATEGIES

**1. Play Aggressively.**

There will be a number of readers who have done well in small home games, who, when they hit the Vegas casinos, get beaten like chumps. They leave the table without their bankroll, shaking their heads, and wondering what went wrong. What usually goes wrong in these situations is that they play the same way they play at home, and it doesn't work in bigger limits against better players.

Here are some common errors that must be corrected. Let's use a game like 7-Card Stud as an example.

**a. The player disguises his hand to sucker in as many players as possible.**

This is one of the worst strategies you can use, for it is doomed to lose you money. For example, suppose you are dealt the following cards at the outset of play:

At home, most players will just call with this hand, hoping to get a bunch of "suckers" to stay in the pot. However, the more players, the weaker the Aces become. If you allow someone in with a small three straight, he may draw out against you. A pair of deuces may turn into a set of three.

The correct play is to immediately raise.

Let's assume we're in Vegas, in a $5-$10 game, where the ante is 50¢ and the low card must **bring it in** (bet) for a dollar. Let's assume that a deuce of diamonds brought it in, a Queen and a 10 called, and everyone else went out, and now the bet is around to you. Raise! You've got to drive out as many players as possible.

For the top pros, the ideal situation in poker is not a royal flush; it's having a pair of Aces against one other player in the game who has to draw out to beat the Aces. Either he has a weaker pair or a pure drawing hand, going for a flush or a straight. That's the ideal situation.

If you raised as suggested, chances are overwhelming that the deuce that brought in the bet will immediately fold, and perhaps either the Queen or the 10 hand will also fold. Let's assume they don't fold. You have two players in against you.

You bet out on Fourth Street, the next card dealt. Without hesitation. If neither had paired, you'll probably find one more going down the drain, and now you're in an ideal situation.

Mediocre players think that you must disguise your hand if you hold a strong opening pair, but the rule is just the opposite. You must raise with them immediately. Suppose, in the previous hand, you raised with your Ace, and the deuce folded but the Queen reraised you.

What do you do? We'll assume the 10 has folded also. You reraise! The Queen probably has just a pair of Queens, or maybe a different pair and never should have reraised unless he thought you were trying to "steal the ante."

There's no deception necessary here. You reraise and by doing this say you have Aces. He should throw away his cards. If he doesn't, he's a fool, and punish him all the way.

**b. A Player will call till Sixth Street or even The River (Seventh Street, the last card dealt). And now, if he's sure he has a winning hand, he'll bet aggressively and raise aggressively.**

This is the way amateurs play. When they get to Vegas, they get worried when no player allows them this kind of stupid leisurely play. Checks come at them from all directions.

The correct play is to be aggressive and raise if you figure you have the top hand and drive out players at once. Only if you have weak cards that need help, such as drawing to a straight or flush, do you want to drift along. Or **limp in**, as the pros say.

In the smaller games in Vegas, you see much the same style as home games. Players with the high card on board will check, and everyone else will check on Fourth Street, then Fifth Street, and on Sixth Street, when some dummy finally shows two open pair, he now bets, and everyone folds and he wins a $4 pot. And wonders why he's a loser at the end of the evening.

**c. A player will check with a sure winning hand at the River, not wanting to squeeze the extra bet from a hapless opponent.**

A better strategy would be to flush the wallet down the toilet. The whole point of professional poker is to get in those extra bets. That separates the top players from the others. The best players, the great ones, know how to maneuver a hand to get in extra bets. They never allow a player to escape without a bet if they can induce another wager.

**d. Players stay in with a *scare card***

Players stay in with a **scare card**, that is a card that's powerful, such as an Ace, King or Queen, because they're ashamed to fold it even though they have garbage underneath. They're afraid to be called a "tight player." Well, who really cares? Suckers and chumps think poker is a game of luck anyway, so it really doesn't matter what you do.

For example, if you hold:

You throw these cards away as soon as possible. They're un-playable unless you are in late position and want to **steal the ante**, that is, reraise and force one or two players who limped in out of the game under the pretense of having a pair of Aces.

But that may be fruitless strategy in most cases. You just want to get rid of the cards because they'll end up costing you money in the long run.

As you shall see, there are several ways to dispel the idea that you're a "tight player," without throwing money down the toilet by playing a hand like this.

### 2. Don't Give Free Cards

During the play of the hand, avoid giving your opponent a free card, while trying to give yourself one as often as feasible. A **free card** is basically a round of play where a player doesn't have to call or make a bet, so the card he gets during that round of play costs him nothing - is **free**.

For most players, the whole idea of a free card is as foreign as Bulgarian cuisine. But it is an important concept and we'll deal in greater length in the appropriate games with this idea.

Here's an example of getting a free card. In 7-Card Stud, as played in casinos, there are two betting levels. For example, in the $10-$20 game, a player can bet $20 only after his Fifth Street card, or on Fourth Street, if an open pair is showing. Suppose that on Fourth Street, where the betting is still in the $10 range, you hold:

There is only one opponent against you. He is showing King of Clubs and has just been dealt the 4 of diamonds. He originally raised with the King and now bets $10. You raise to $20. He calls.

On Fifth Street he now shows:

You have:

You had figured him for either a pair with the King kicker, or a pair of Kings. Your raise with the 10 of clubs made him think. Do you have two pair? He hasn't improved. In fact the deuce of hearts was probably a disaster. So he checks his King "to the raiser." You check behind him. On Fifth Street where bets are twice as expensive, you've gotten yourself a free card.

Now any kind of scare card, such as a club or Jack and he'll check and might throw away his hand on Sixth Street if he gets another **rag** (useless card).

The converse of the situation may present itself. You don't want to let your opponent get a free card. It's almost axiomatic for a good player to bet if the opponent first checks to him. You may win the pot outright, or you may put so much fear into the opponent that any scare card that seems to help you on the next Street will force him to throw away his hand.

Never give him a free card to beat you with. Make him pay for this privilege. Weak players in small games give away three free cards in a round of play, till the opponent draws out on them and beats them. Good players always are on the lookout for free cards and never give them to opponents.

## 3. Raise, Don't Call

In many situations, you want to raise, not call a bet. There's an expression that jaded poker pros use for players who constantly call bets. They're known as **calling stations**. They're the easiest players in the world to beat because they never put you under pressure. They'll call and call and if they hit or draw a miracle card, then they'll raise, usually on the River. Then, you can simply throw your cards away. You can read these players like a book.

On the other hand, strong pros are constantly in there raising, from the getgo. They'll either fold or raise, or else they won't bother with the action. I know a very successful pro like this, who started with a few hundred dollars when he came to Vegas and now has several hundred thousand dollars, all from poker winnings.

He raises and reraises. When it comes to him, the other players cringe, because if he's in, it's going to cost them heavy money. Once, he told me slyly, he was dealt three Aces rolled up in 7-card stud, and merely called the bet. Everyone started laughing at the table. "Hey, man, we know what you got. Three Aces?" And they were right. So if he's playing, and he feels he may have the strongest hand, he's in there raising.

Sometimes you want to limp in. This happens with drawing hands, where you need to buy a card or two to form the flush or straight. You would call in those spots. But if you're in the lead, bet and then reraise. Maintain this aggressive pose - it pays dividends in poker.

### 4. Take control of the table.

You should be the one the other players fear. You should make them cringe. Be aggressive and have them wince every time you're raising. However, the higher stakes you play, the better the opposition, and there will be others at the table doing just that.

I asked a pro what it was like to play against one of the legendary 7-card stud players, and he said that you could never make him back down. You raised him, you were reraised, and if you reraised, he came right back at you. That eventually translates to fear if he's winning. He'll roll over any table with that attitude.

### 5. Practice deception.

Great players have a saying. "I play the opponent's cards, not mine." Or "I put the opponent on a hand, and play against that hand." That's called "reading an opponent."

You can't afford to allow yourself to be read simply. The chumps make it easy. For example, in most small limit games, their idea of deception is to throw money aggressively in, "splashing it," as they say, when they're weak, and halfheartedly yet when they have monster hands.

For example, I was playing against one of the locals in Vegas, and he'd say, "one more heart and you're in trouble." So, immediately I knew he didn't have a draw to a heart flush. If another heart came out and I got a rag, and couldn't win anyway, I'd throw away my cards and say, "Kings up isn't going to beat that flush." And he'd arch his eyebrows as would every other local at the table. It was a joke, and the joke was on them.

In the smaller games, if a player drops in his chips with a wary gesture and says "I'm in this far, I might as well see another card," you'd be best advised to get out right then and there. He probably has a formed winning hand already.

If he splashes his chips aggressively, I usually would recommend an immediate reraise. These guys are playing infant poker, and are as subtle as Jack the Ripper.

However, in the bigger games against better players, it isn't that simple to figure out hands. Some of these players are professionals, and have perfected various moves over the lifetime of their poker career. They try and set other players up for deceptive moves. If they've raised steadily only on strong hands, they may now change gears and slow play a big hand.

By **slow play** we mean not raise but limp in with the big hand. **Fast play** is aggressive raising poker; slow play is the opposite. It has nothing to do with how fast or slow the gambler plays his cards in terms of speed.

Or they may fast play mediocre hands with good drawing possibilities, something weaker players hardly ever do. These good players try and avoid "tells" against them, that is, moves that signal clearly what their cards are. Though they occassionally alter their play, a number of locals with professional aspirations usually play the same type of game, good enough to beat the tourists in Vegas casinos, but not good enough against really fine, strong players.

As for yourself, don't let your gestures give your hand away. .

Don't fall into predictable patterns against strong players in big games. Alter your moves. We'll discuss this strategy when we deal with specific games.

**6. Study your opposition.**

You can't be a winner just playing your own cards and disregarding what your opponents are doing. Even if you have an evening of marvellous cards and win a great number of pots, you still want to make the most of the situation, get in extra bets, build up big pots for yourself.

During the course of a session of poker, you must be alert at all times, and this includes the times you are out of the pot.

Watch the other players; study their moves and gestures. Is anything giving them away? It could be something as simple as lifting up a bunch of chips when they intend only to call a bet. If they intend to raise, they wait without holding chips in their hands. A lot of players do this - thinking it's clever and frightening to their opposition.

For example, to call the bet requires two checks and they hold four checks in their hand as if to raise, and then drop two checks, calling the bet. It's a beautiful tell and the fools who practice this unsubtle deception don't realize it.

**Playing Against the Animal**

Some players you'll be up against are like animals, raising every pot no matter what they have, trying to drive out other players, and hopefully, if they have decent cards, trying to build up huge pots for themselves.

When you're up against one or two of these animals at the table, don't take control of the game. Go along with them. Let them bet for you, let them build up the pot for you.

For example, you had a hidden pair of Jacks on Third Street, and after getting a rag on Fourth Street, you get another Jack on Fifth Street, so your hand shows:

The wild man at the table has been raising from the outset with a 10 as his **door card** (the card open on Third Street) and now holds:

Another player is in the game. He holds:

Since the Ace didn't reraise the wild man with the 10 of clubs, you put him on either a flush draw or a small pair with Ace kicker, or possibly three high cards, two of them buried. He checks, you can check now, knowing you won't be giving away a free card because the animal will bet, which he does with his 10 and 7 showing. The Ace calls, you raise.

Against normal players, you'd just call, waiting to **pop** (raise) him on Sixth Street, but the animal knows he plays wildly and figures you for a pair of Jacks, beating his 10s. He holds stronger cards, maybe even a set of 10s now, which is perfect for you, so he jams you again. The Ace hesitates and folds, and you can call. You've gotten in a few bets.

If both you and the animal pair on the board now, it looks like this:

**You:**

**Animal:**

This probably means you both have full houses, but yours is a tad better. Now with only two of you in the pot, you can get in a few raises and reraises.

You're representing at least trip 4s here, and he figures he has you beaten. If he was smart, he'd have respected that raise on Fourth Street with the Jack, but he figures you didn't respect his cards, and now he has a big hand and he wants to really punish you, but he's only going to punish himself.

**Playing Against the Rock**

Some players are the opposite of the animal. They are extremely cautious and throw away hands one after the other, hardly ever playing anything but very strong hands. They're known disparingly as **rocks** in the poker world.

If they're in a pot, unless you're extremely strong yourself, let them have the pot. In the California casinos, rocks abound. They are locals who try and grind out some extra money this way. Usually they're older men with time on their hands who've studied poker somewhat and figure there are always some wild men they can feast off at any given table.

The thing to do with rocks is trap them with a monster hand. When you have a full house down the river, when you see only a flush draw in their hands, check to them and then raise them when they bet. Always get that extra bet off rocks. It's easy to do.

So, if you're in a poker game, where most or all of the players are strangers, you have to be alert to their game. Look for tells, look to see when they are about to become aggressive with a bet. Study their styles. It can often make the difference between winning and losing.

Above all, even when you're out of the pot, try and put the

players betting on various hands. See how close you come. If you're wrong, study what they turn over at the showdown. Get a feel for their game and their temperament. It'll stand you in very good stead.

# IV. RANKING OF POKER HANDS.

**HIGH POKER**

We'll briefly show the rankings of hands. For experienced players, this material may be superfluous, but for players not familiar with poker who want to become experts, they should study this section carefully.

**Five of a kind**

A Five of a Kind hand can only occur with the aid of a **joker** or **bug.** Both are the same thing and mean an extra card inserted in the deck which can be usually used as any card.

For example, if you hold:

You have five nines, a Five of a Kind hand. This takes preference over any other hand, including Royal Flushes.

(Only certain games use a joker or a bug.)

**Royal Flush**

Without a bug or wild card which can stand for any card, this is the strongest of all poker hands. It consists of the Ace, King, Queen, Jack and 10 of the same suit. For example:

In other words an Ace high straight flush. It doesn't matter what suit you have the Royal Flush in. In poker all suits are equal, and a Royal Flush in spades is no stronger than a Royal Flush in clubs.

**Straight Flush**

A straight flush consists of five cards in consecutive ranking order, all of the same suit. The following hand is a straight flush:

One straight flush can beat another if the highest card is of higher rank than the highest card of the other straight flush. Thus the straight flush we illustrated will beat a straight flush headed by a 9 in a different suit.

The lowest possible straight flush is:

In this instance, the Ace counts as a one. Any straight flush headed by a 6 or higher will beat this one.

**Four of a Kind**

All four cards of the same rank constitute a Four of a Kind hand.

The fifth card is immaterial here. Another four of a kind hand with higher ranking cards, such as an 8 or above in the example shown, will beat a different four of a kind hand.

The highest is four Aces, the lowest, four 2s.

## Full House

This hand consists of three similar ranking cards plus a pair.

When calling this hand, it is *Threes over Kings*, or *threes full of Kings*. The key cards here are the threes or **treys** as they are known in poker parlance. The **trips** or **set** (three of a kind) determines the ultimate value of the hand, with the pair secondary.

Thus, a Full House with three 4s will beat the full house with three 3s. The pair is not taken into consideration when determining which Full House beats another. Thus:

is weaker than:

That is because the 7s are higher ranked than the 6s in the set. The pair is not used to determine rank.

## Flush

A flush consists of five cards, all of the same suit.

This is a spade Flush. If there are two or more flushes in one game, then the flush with the highest ranking card wins the pot, or if those are tied, the second ranked determines the winner and so forth. The above flush would be called as a "ten high flush." Any flush headed by a Jack or higher ranked card will beat the 10 high flush.

## Straight

This hand consists of five cards in sequence, of different suits. The highest straight is led by the Ace as the high card:

The lowest is:

When two players both have straights, the hand headed by the highest ranked cards wins the pot. Thus an 8 high straight will beat out a 7 high straight.

## Three of a Kind

This hand consists of a set plus two odd cards.

This is a Three of a Kind hand, three Queens. If two players hold three of a kind hands, the highest ranking one wins.

Sometimes, where there are community cards such as in Texas Hold 'em, two or more player can have the same three of a kind hand. In that case, the highest ranking odd card in a player's hand determines the winner. For example, in the above situation we see three Queens with a 6 and a 2. If in Hold 'em, another player had three Queens plus any odd card over a 6 in rank, he would win the pot.

In all our discussions of two hands holding the same kinds of poker hands, we assume that they are the best hands, and will win the pot. For example, if two players hold Three of a Kind hands but another holds a Flush, then the Flush hand wins. However if the Three of a Kind hands are the strongest at the showdown, then they are compared for higher ranking trips.

## Two Pair

This hand consists of two separate pairs plus an odd or fifth card, which may, in some instances, have value.

This is a two pair hand, "8s over 6s." If there is another two pair hand with a higher pair than 8s, the other hand will win. Thus "9s over deuces" will beat the illustrated hand.

Very rarely will two players have the same two pairs in most games of poker, though it frequently happens in Texas Hold 'em. Then the fifth or odd card comes into play.

Suppose two players hold Kings over Jacks, but one player's odd card is a Queen and the other's is a 10. The following hand consisting of:

beats the previous hand with the 10 as an odd card, since the Queen is higher ranked than the 10.

## One Pair

A single pair with three odd cards characterize this hand. An example would be:

If two players have identical pairs, then the highest odd card among the three remaining cards determines the winner. If that odd card is identical in rank in two hands, we go to the next odd card. Thus a pair of Kings with an Ace will beat a pair of Kings with a Queen as the highest odd card.

## No Pair

The weakest of all poker hands. This kind of hand consists of five odd cards. If two players remain at the showdown, both with five odd cards, then the player holding the highest odd card wins.

Thus a hand headed by a Jack will beat one headed by a ten. If the two hands have identically ranked high cards, we look at the second highest card to determine the winner. If that is also identical, we go to the third and so forth, until we determine a winner.

## LOBALL POKER

In loball Poker, the object of the game is to have the lowest possible hand. This is diametrically opposite from high poker, in which the highest ranked hand wins the pot.

In Loball, flushes and straights are disregarded and do not foul the hand or make it a high hand. What is important and counts is the rank of the highest card in the hand. In this regard, an Ace can always be considered a low card, counting as a 1, at the option of the player. Thus a hand of 8 7 6 3 Ace, would be an 8-7 low hand, with the Ace counting as a 1.

## The Wheel or Bicycle

In most games of loball, unless another hand is specifically mentioned as the lowest, a perfect hand is the **Wheel**. It consists of the 5 4 3 2 Ace. It is the best hand and beats every other hand but another wheel.

This is the second best hand.

In some loball games, played usually in private homes, this is the best hand, when straights and flushes count against a low hand. In these instances the wheel then would be considered a straight.

However, in practically all loball games you'll encounter, the wheel will be best, with the 6-4 the second best. I call it a 6-4 because that is how one describes a low hand, naming the top two cards in rank.

After the 6 4 3 2 Ace, we have a 6 5 3 2 A and then a 6 5 4 2 Ace and so forth. Any 6 low beats a 7 low. Any 7 low beats an 8 low.

Sometimes a hand is won in loball by a pair or higher. If this occurs at the showdown, the lower pair of two competing hands would win. A single pair will beat two pair. If the pairs are identical, the player holding the *lowest* odd card wins.

In other words, it is the exact opposite of high poker.

# V. BASIC ASPECTS OF POKER

### Players' Deals

In some games in the California clubs, and in practically all games played in private homes, the players deal, without the use of a professional dealer.

When the players deal, the deal moves around the table in a clockwise fashion, so that each player has the right to deal. Sometimes a player refuses or can't deal and someone else deals for him or her. In that event, no matter where the designated dealer deals from, the player to the left of the person who should have dealt receives the first card.

Before the cards are dealt, they should be shuffled thoroughly by the dealer, and then handed to the player to his or her right to be cut. Then the cards are replaced in a final stack and dealt out.

For most poker games, the first card off the top of the deck is dealt to the player to the dealer's left, and then one card each, all face down, is dealt to the next player in turn and so forth, till each player at the table gets a card in clockwise fashion. The last person to receive a card is always the dealer.

Then, depending on the game, another card is dealt in the same manner. In games like 7-Card Stud, each player will receive two cards face down and one face up, the third card being dealt face up.

### Stud Games

In the Stud games, after the initial two or three cards have been dealt out, the **stock** (the remaining cards in the deck not yet dealt) is put to one side by the dealer. After the first round of play is over, with all bets made, then the dealer picks up the stock and deals another card, face up, to each player remaining in the round of play.

This process is repeated till each player has his or her full complement of cards. After all the cards necessary have been dealt out, the stock is put to one side, not to be used again. After the game is over, the cards are gathered up by the new dealer, shuffled up, and given to the previous dealer, the player on his right, to be cut. Then the game continues with the new dealer dealing out the cards.

### Draw Poker

In draw poker, there are two rounds of play. In the first, all five cards are dealt face down by the dealer, one at a time to each player. Then the stock is put aside till the next round of play. After the **draw**, when each player asks for cards, the cards are dealt in a clump, that is, if a player asks for three cards, all three cards are dealt to him face down at one time. This contrasts with the deal before the draw, when one card is dealt at a time to each player in tun.

### Hold 'em

In games like Hold 'em where there are community cards, the deal is slightly different. Each player in that game gets two cards face down, dealt one at a time in clockwise fashion. Then there's a round of betting. Now the dealer deals out the **flop**, which is the first three cards put on the board to be used as community cards by all the players remaining in the game.

However, before he does this, he **burns**, (deals the first card face down and out of play, to one side) the top card, then puts out three cards face up to the flop. Then a fourth card is put up on the board face up after a round of betting and after the top card is burned. Then the last card is put up in the same manner after the top card is burned.

That basically takes care of home deals where players deal their own cards.

In California casinos, in certain games, there might be other rules. After each round of dealing out cards, the dealer must cap the deck, that is, put a chip on the deck or stock while it stands in one side. Before playing in California clubs where the players deal the cards, learn the rules of dealing in the game. A misdeal can cost you the pot if you screw up.

**Professional Casino Dealers**

In all the stud games and Hold 'em games, plus some others in California casinos, and in all the Vegas casino poker games, a professional dealer will be in charge of dealing out the cards. The players have no say in this. Here's how it works:

The dealer will have two decks of cards in a tray in front of him or her, along with checks for use by players in case they want to exchange cash for chips or checks (same thing).

He uses one deck at a time. In games like Stud Poker, where position at the table isn't important, since low card opens the betting, the dealer will shuffle up the cards and cut them himself. Then he will deal out the cards in clockwise fashion. The spot to his left, the first player to get a card, is known as the **1 Seat**. The last player to receive a card at a full table, the player to his right, is in the **8 Seat**.

After each round of dealing, the cards remain in the dealer's hand while bets are made. Then he continues to deal the next round and so forth, till all rounds are played and there is a showdown. Then the cards are gathered in by the dealer, who continually takes in discards as the game is played and puts them down to one side.

In Hold 'em and Draw Poker, since position is of extreme importance, a **button** is moved around the table in clockwise fashion after every deal. The man **on the button** is the theoretical dealer as far as betting goes, and acts last, an enormous advantage in Hold 'em and Draw Poker.

In the Draw Poker games, where a dealer is used, he deals the cards face down in the first round of play till all players have five cards, and then after the draw, deals the cards to the players in clumps, so that, if a player wants three cards, he gets them all at once off the top of the deck.

In the course of a poker game, any player can request the changing of one deck for the other deck in the tray after a round of play ends. Or a player may ask for a new **setup** which is a new set of two decks of cards, replacing the ones in the dealer's tray.

In the games where the professional dealer is used, he or she runs the game, announcing who bets first, what the bet should be, and so forth. If there is any dispute between two players or a player and the dealer, a **floorman** may be called over to resolve it. He is the supervisor and his word is final.

### The Ante Structure

Although many amateurs and weak players don't pay attention to the ante structure, the better players and pros use this as a guide to determine their style of play at the poker table.

The **ante** is defined as money or chips put into the pot prior to the deal of the cards, in order to increase the value or **sweeten** the pot. This money remains in the pot whether or not any player decides to fold, that is, throw away or discard his hand.

In many home games there is no ante in stud poker, and the same holds true in some of the smaller games found in Las Vegas casinos. For instance, in a $1-$4 game, there is no ante in many of the casinos that feature this limit game.

When there is no ante, it encourages tight players who slow play their hands, that is, don't raise at the outset and limp along to the later streets. There's no sense in making a big bet at the outset, on Third Street in stud poker, if everyone folds. All you get back is your big bet and possibly some poor guy's previous $1 bet.

Where the ante is 10% of the minimum bet, we're talking about a normal ante. Thus, in a $5-$10 game, the ante of 50¢ in the Vegas casinos is normal. However, in the California clubs there is a $1 ante in the same limit game, and this is moderately high. In

40

the bigger Vegas games, such as the $100-$200 game, the ante is $25, which makes it quite high.

The higher the ante, the faster the play, the earlier the betting and raising and reraising. The smaller the ante in proportion to the bet, the slower the play, with bettors hesitating to make early raises. Thus, in these small or no ante games, the early Streets are usually bet and call situations.

However, sometimes the ante structure just punishes the players and doesn't alter the play. Let's take the $5-$10 game in the California clubs. There is a $1 ante, which means that eight players put out $1 each, or $8. However, the dealer takes $3.50 of that immediately, leaving just $4.50 out on the table. The player has been forced to ante a big proportion of his initial bet, yet he has no benefit from the higher ante structure.

In addition, in the California clubs there is a $2 bring in by low card, which means that the low card showing on Third Street must bet $2. This is twice as high as the Vegas clubs' bring in, which is $1 in a $5-$10 game.

It's very difficult with this peculiar structure to win at the $5-$10 game in the California clubs. Despite the high ante structure, we have slow playing, for there's really no reason to fast play a hand.

With the high ante structure and slow playing situation, with the high bring in, the game neither benefits the player who likes to play tight, or the loose player. Both will suffer with this structure.

When there is a big ante, or high ante structure, there is a definite reason why the game is fast played.

Let's look at the difference between a $10-$20 game and a $100-$200 game. One would think that the $100 game is exactly 10 times a big as the $10 game, but that's not the case at all. In the 7-Card Stud game, $10-$20, each player antes $1, or 10% of the minimum bet. There is now $8 on the table. Low hand brings it in for $2. Now we have $10 on the table.

In a place like the Mirage Hotel and Casino in Vegas, a popular place to play poker, the first raise can be $7, rather than $10. Thus, with $10 in the pot already ($8 in antes and the $2 bring in) a player can try and steal the ante by betting $7. He gets $10 for his $7 bet if all players go out. This is a 1.43-1 approximate ratio. A worthwhile try. If a player reraises, he'll have to put in $17 ($7 plus a $10 raise) but there's only $17 in the pot now, and he'll get 1-1 for his money. This reraise, except for strategic purposes in driving out players, isn't that worthwhile just to steal an ante.

Let's now look at the $100-$200 game. Each player antes $25 or 25% of the minimum bet. A very high ante. Thus, there's $200 in the pot before the cards are dealt. Low card brings it in for $25. Now there's $225 in the pot. It certainly pays for a bettor to put out a $100 bet to try and win $225. He's getting 2.25-1. Now, with $325 in the pot ($200 in antes, $25 bring in and $100 raise) another player can easily bet $200 to try and win $325. He's getting 1.625-1 for his bet. And a third player who now raises it to $300 is getting $525 for his $300 bet or a greater 1.75-1 for his bet.

So, we find that in a $10-$20 game, there is usually one raise to $7, plus the $2 bring in and the $8 ante for a total of $17 in the pot or 1.7 times the minimum bet. Even with another raise, which is rare, the pot contains $27 or 2.7 times the minimum bet.

Compare this with the $100-$200 game, where often on Third Street there's $825 on the pot for an 8.25-1 ration, and even without that capping (final) third raise, there's still $525 in the pot for a 5.25-1 ratio.

A player who is tight, who likes to slow play, will be buried alive in the $100-$200 game. The bigger the game, the wilder the ante structure, the faster the play.

And as an anomaly, the weaker the hands that win. In the big games, a pair can take the pot whereas in the smaller game, at least two pair is necessary. The reason for this is simple - in the big games with the high ante structure, players must go in with weaker cards to survive, otherwise the ante will eat them up.

In a $100-$200 game, every four hands of anteing will equal a minimum bet, whereas in the $10-$20 game every ten antes will equal a minimum bet.

This unequal ante structure is one of the main reasons why players, when moving up in poker to bigger games, find that it gets tougher to play these games. There's stronger competition, and faster play. If you can beat both, you can be a big winner. And that's what our discussion of advanced poker is all about, showing you how to be comfortable no matter what the ante structure, and how to play to win.

**Betting Limits**

In the smaller games of poker, there may be a wide spread of betting options, particularly in the 7-Stud games. For example, in the $1-$4 game, one can bet from the minimum to the maximum on all betting rounds, including anything in between. Sometimes there's a $1-$4 with an $8 bet on the river after all the cards are dealt. Sometimes there's even $1-$5 games.

We mention these games in passing because we don't recommend them. We say this for a variety of reasons.

First of all, if you know poker, you want to play bigger games to win more money at them. Secondly, there's the matter of the rake. The **rake** is the money removed from the pot by the house dealer during every game.

In the smaller games it can amount to 10% or more. In bigger games, the rake is either 5% or a set amount of money, which ever is less. For example, no matter how big the pot in a $5-$10 7-Stud game, only $2.50 can be raked.

In the very big games, usually starting with the $15-$30 games, there's usually an hourly fee charged to the players, with no rake. This holds true for the bigger games in the California clubs, which have higher fees than the Vegas casinos.

Other than the smallest games, there's usually a two-tiered betting limit, with the bottom figure one-half of the top figure. Thus the game will be $5-$10 or $15-$30 or $50-$100 or $2,000-$4,000. There are also no-limit games, but this book is geared to the limit games.

In draw poker games, the minimum bet is made on the first

round, and the maximum on the second round. Thus, in a $10-$20 draw Loball game, the bets will be $10 before the draw and $20 after.

In the Stud games, there usually will be an opening bet by low hand, called **bringing it in.** This is usually double the ante or equal to the ante, depending on the game. In the smaller games it is double, in the bigger games, it is equal, though there are variations on this as well. But that's the general rule.

In 7-Stud, the first three cards are dealt, prior to the first bet and at this point, is known as Third Street. After the bring in, a raise will usually be the minimum bet. For example, in a $15-$30 game, after the bring in, the raise makes it $15.

On Third Street and Fourth Street in the same type of game, the bets and raises are at the bottom tier, the minimum. Thus, after the $15 raise, someone else can raise to $30 by making an additional $15 bet. The same holds true on Fourth Street, where high card must bet or check, and the first bet is $15, with $15 increments in raises.

However, if there's an open pair on Fourth Street, then the player holding the high hand can either bet $15 or $30. This option is true in the other 7-Stud limit games. Even if the high hand decides to bet only $15, another player can raise by $30. This is a unique situation, happening only on Fourth Street. Thereafter, on the later streets; Fifth, Sixth and Seventh (The River), bets and raises are at the high end of the tier. Thus in the $15-$30 game, the raises will be in $30 increments after a $30 bet.

In Hold 'em games, there is also a two-tiered structure that is rather strict, with no options as were seen in the 7-Stud games. Let's say the game is $5-$10. There is a **blind** usually in these games, equal to the minimum bet. Sometimes there are two blinds. A blind is a bet that must be made regardless of the cards the player holds, because of his position in the game.

Thus, the player who is the blind is the player to the left of the theoretical dealer, the one who has the button. He must bet $5, and each subsequent player must call or raise the bet to stay in. No one can check without **checking out,** that is, folding his cards and getting out of the game. When it comes around to the blind, he can raise if he desires or stand on his original bet, assuming no one else has raised. This is known as a **live blind.**

If there has been a raise or raises before it gets to the blind's turn again, he can either match the raise, reraise or fold.

The betting on the flop is still at the same tier as the betting before the flop, the minimum bet. Now the blind can check instead of being forced to bet. The bets are now in the lower tier range with raises the same way. On the next card dealt, Fourth Street, bets are in the maximum range, as they are on Fifth Street, with all raises in the same range.

Thus, if the betting range is $5-$10 in a Hold 'em game, on Fourth Street a bet must be $10, and a raise must be to $20. No bets in between are allowed.

What if a player in any game runs out of checks? He can still be in the game, after making his bet and announcing "all in", but bets after his will be segregated into another pot that he can't win. Two separate pots will exist on the table.

The player "all in" can only win the pot he's contributed checks to, while the side pot will be won by some other player, even if the other player has an inferior hand.

### Raising Limits

In the California clubs, the raises are limited to three when there are more than two players in the game. This is to prevent collusion among two players who trap a third one into endless raises. In the Vegas poker rooms, some games will have three raise limits, others as many as four. When only two players remain in the game, the raises are unlimited.

### Check and Raise

**Check and raise** is also permitted in California and Vegas poker rooms. This is a fairly universal rule. It means that, after checking initially, a player may come in for a subsequent raise. Be aware of this rule when playing these clubs, and in private games as well.

# VI. SEVEN-CARD STUD - HIGH

## Introduction

In Seven-Card Stud, three of the seven cards are dealt face down, hidden from the other players. This makes the game rather complex, since, to figure out the unknown cards, the astute player must study the betting patterns and understand the strength and/or weakness of the opponent. Psychology enters the picture as well, because those three unseen cards give a good player a great deal of leverage in his betting and raising moves.

Although Hold 'em has supplanted 7-Stud as the most popular of the casino and club games, it is still the favorite game of players whose poker action is in private games. Because of the seven cards dealt, many players feel that this is primarily a game of luck, but that's not the case at all.

Anyone can get lucky, but skill remains the constant, the benchmark which determines winners and losers in the long run. As you study the intricacies of this game and master them, you'll be able to play any poker game well. Whether playing in a casino, club or at home, skill in this game will pay off in winning dividends.

## The Street and Rounds of Betting

Experienced casino players refer to streets rather than rounds of play. At the outset of play, the dealer will deal out three cards, the first two down and the third face up. At this point, we're at **Third Street**, named for the three cards already held by each player. From there we go to Fourth, Fifth, Sixth and finally Seventh Street, also known as **The River**.

For purposes of this section, our main discussion will hinge on the casino game as played in Las Vegas, where there is a house dealer, and the rules are slightly different from the home game.

The main difference occurs on Third Street.

In home games, the high hand bets first and usually bets the lower tier of whatever the game is. Thus, in a $5-$10 game, he will bet $5 and open the betting this way.

However, in Vegas, low card opens the betting, or brings it in. The bet in a $5-$10 wouldn't be $5, but $1 .Or he may open with $5. This is rarely done, for generally, the low card doesn't have much of a hand to start with and is happy to just bet this low amount of $1.

The purpose of having a low card open the betting is to force some kind of action, and to sweeten the pot so that stealing the ante becomes worthwhile. By **stealing the ante**, we mean attempting by a raise to force all the other players out on Third Street to win whatever is in the pot, which would be the antes and the opener's bet.

This is a standard ploy in casino poker, for the antes add up, and it also enables the raiser to force other players out, even if he can't steal the ante right then and there.

Since there is a house dealer, who always gives the first card to the player to his left, known as the **first seat**, and the last card to the player on his right, known as the **eighth seat**, if two players have identical low cards, the opener is determined by the value of the suits.

The lowest suit is clubs, then diamonds, hearts and finally spades, the highest suit. Thus, if two players had received open deuces on Third Street, the lowest suit value deuce would bring it in. A 2 of clubs would open the betting if any other deuce were exposed. This is to prevent position at the table from being an advantage.

After Third Street, the suits have no intrinsic value in casino poker. Thereafter, high hand opens the betting on all later streets.

Once the opener has bet, all other players must match the bet or raise to stay in the pot. If you check after someone opens, you check out, and fold your cards.

In a $5-$10 game, for example, after it's brought in for $1, the next player to bet, the one to the left of the opener, can call the bet, raise to $5 or fold. The raises must adhere to the game, and no raises between $1 and $5 is permitted. Thereafter the players act in turn, either calling, raising or folding.

Only three raises are permitted on any one round if there are three or more players in the game. With two players, raising is unlimited and can go on till the players run out of money. This rule is in to prevent collusion between two players working as a team who trap another player and raise and reraise until the other, third player, runs out of money.

Also, **check and raise** is permitted in practically all casino and club games. A player may check his hand and then raise when it is his turn to bet again. This will only occur on Fourth Street and later streets, since the low card on Third Street can't check.

On Fourth Street the highest hand now opens the betting and this rule follows for all subsequent streets. He may now check and not be out of the game. The betting on Third and Fourth Streets is still in the lower tier of betting, and in a $5-$10 game would be $5 and increments of $5.

However, there is one exception to this rule. If a player shows an open pair on Fourth Street he must bet $5 or $10 if he is the opener. Even if he bets $5, someone else can raise by $10. This can only occur on Fourth Street.

Fifth Street and subsequent streets are in the high tier of betting, the **expensive streets**.

Here, in a $5-$10 game, the betting is $10 and increments of $10. Of course, all the players can check on any round from Fourth Street on and there would be no betting. On Sixth Street, each player will now have two cards down and four up. After this round of betting, we come to Seventh Street, the River. After this round of betting there is the **showdown**. Those remaining in the game now show cards to determine the winner of the pot.

The player **called**, the one who bet or raised first, shows his cards. The others, if they think they beat his hand, can show theirs for this purpose, or they may concede the pot and not show cards.

When the caller shows his cards, he must show all seven, not his five best. If any other player shows his cards to win the pot, he also must show all seven. The cards **speak for themselves.** A player may overlook a flush, for example and think he has only two pair. It is up to the dealer to correct this, if the player announces "two pair."

The best thing to do is simply to show all your cards and let the dealer sort out your best hand, without you saying anything.

Once you throw away your cards and it goes into the **muck pile**, the pile of discarded cards, you cannot claim the pot anymore. So, when in doubt, just show your cards. Sometimes you may overlook a winning hand after a long night of poker.

### The Ante Structure

In home games, which we'll go into in a smaller way, there usually is no ante in stud games. Sometimes the dealer puts in a small ante, but it really plays no part in the general betting scheme, and certainly is not something worth going after or stealing.

However, in the casino game, all players (except for the really small games in some casinos, such as $1-$4) put in an ante before every game. The normal ante is 10% of the minimum bet in games like $5-$10 and $10-$20, moving up to $3 in the $15-$30 games (20%) to a big 25% in the $100-$200 games.

The bigger the ante in proportion to the bets, the more action will take place, and the faster the betting. Again, to refresh our recollection, *fast play* means that there are more raises, not some speed of betting test. *Slow play*, on the other hand, means fewer raises and more calls.

The 10% difference between the $10-$20 game and the $15-$30 game means a world of difference. If there is a dividing line in casino poker, it is the $15-$30 game which separates the serious men from the boys.

If you can beat $15-$30, you can move up to $20-$40, $30-$60 and into the higher stratospheres of $50-$100 and so on. These are scary games in terms of money to be risked, and you must know how to play poker to hold your own against players at this level.

If you like to play tight, and feel uncomfortable with a lot of raises at the outset, then you're not going to be able to play $15-$30 or beyond. But if you learn poker correctly, it should be no problem.

For the moment, we'll concentrate on the $10-$20 game, risky enough, to show the fine points of 7-Stud that will enable you to be a winner.

The important thing to remember is this; know that the ante determines the speed of play, and play accordingly. To most amateurs, the ante is just a nuisance; to the pros, it's often the difference between winning and losing, in terms of how many antes they can steal.

The bigger the ante in proportion to the game, the more it's worth stealing. But even at 10%, it's worth grabbing now and then. Antes add up, and not only that, aggressive play helps your game, as we shall see.

## Third Street Play

By far, this is the most important street in 7-Stud. Your decision here is to stay in the game or fold your cards immediately. Once that decision is made, should you merely call or raise, or if raised, reraise?

If you can't make correct decisions at Third Street, you're doomed to lose. If you stay in with poor cards, you'll end up chasing stronger hands and you'll be punished for it. If you slow play strong pairs, you'll end up being outdrawn a lot of times by weaker hands that were allowed to limp in for small bets.

First of all, let's discuss the hands you should stay in with at Third Street.

## Minimum Playable Hands and Position

Position at the table counts in 7-stud. A late position hand can be weaker than an early position hand, and still be payable. For now, we'll discuss position and its role in minimum playable hands. By position, we mean the betting position at the table. **Early position** is the opener and the first or second seat after him. **Middle position** is the fourth, fifth or sixth player. Seventh and eighth position is **late position**.

An example: Let's suppose you're in seat #8. The player in seat #1 has a deuce of clubs and must open. He bets $2 in a $10-$20 game, and one by one the players fold except for a player in seat #6 who limps in with the $2 bet. Player #7 folds and that leaves you. Now you can stay in with a variety of hands you would have to fold if you were in early position or even middle position.

You can even raise if your **door card** (the exposed card) is a scare card (a high card here). A raise might even win the pot for you outright.

So, suppose you hold the following:

The King is your doorcard. Player #6 limped in with an 8 of spades. You raise, and the deuce folds, and most probably the 8 of spades will fold. If he stays in for the raise, and you get any kind of scare card on the next round, say **paint** (Jack, Queen or King) or an Ace and bet out, and he gets a **blank** (worthless card), he'll probably fold.

On the other hand, if player #7 opened with a deuce and you were first to act after him, there's no future with your cards. You'd be better off folding. Calling is useless, for it would allow others to limp in after you, and a raise may possibly come from another player. There's really no sense in seeing the raise, putting good money after bad.

If you raise at the outset, if there is no card higher than a King on board, you may steal the ante, but if a few players call the raise, or you're reraised you're in trouble. A reraise and you should throw your cards away.

That's how important position is, and why it must be a consideration in playing 7-Stud, and determining what you should do on Third Street.

Let's now look at various hands that should be played on Third Street, starting with the best.

## Trips

A set, or three-of-a-kind, are the best cards you can receive. Usually, they're winners without any improvement to the River. It'll take a drawing hand to beat them, such as a potential flush or straight, or, in rare cases, a higher set or a full house.

Trips should be played slowly, for your interest is in building up the pot and keeping as many players as possible in the game. They're easy to disguise and no one assumes you have a set.

Suppose you have 9s **rolled up**, that is, a set of 9s on Third Street. You're in fairly early position, for the opener is just before you. You merely call the $1 bet, and wait to see what happens. Suppose there's another call by a Queen of clubs, and a raise by an Ace of spades. What do you do? You merely call the raise. If the Queen also calls, great. You want three way action here, for that means more bets and more money in the pot. You won't start raising till Fifth Street in this situation.

Sometimes, with trips, you can raise on Third Street. Suppose you have trip Kings, a truly monster hand. You're in late position, and after a deuce opened, a 10 called and an Ace also called. You raise. It is a logical move, attempting to get out players and possibly steal the ante. If the Ace has been playing possum and now reraises you, you just call. What you're telling him is - you know he has Aces and you merely have Kings and have to respect him. A reraise here might give away your hand, and he might just concede to you right then and there.

The key is slowplaying the trips. They should end up as winners whether or not you improve them. Obviously, sometimes the trips won't improve and will get beaten by another hand. But your best bet is to slowplay them, unless as in the previous example, you're in a position where your raise, even on Third Street, won't give away your strength.

## The Premium Pairs

10s or better are premium pairs. This includes 10s, Jacks, Queens, Kings and Aces. Of course, Aces are your best premium pair, because no other pair can beat them, and Aces up, assuming no other player also has Aces up, forces a player to have at least trips to beat you.

When you have the premium pair, you must play them differently than smaller and weaker pairs. The basic first rule with the premium pair is to immediately raise.

What you want to do is winnow out the field against you, so that the premium pair, aided possibly by another pair, will win the pot for you. Even if your raise forces everyone out, you haven't lost anything. You've won a small pot, but it's still a pot.

What you don't want to do is limp in with a premium pair, allowing two or three players to stay in with you who would ordinarily fold if you raised right away. They are really getting a free card on Fourth Street. In a $10-$20 game, all it costs them is $2 to see the next card, not $10.

Suppose you didn't raise, and the opener, who had to bet with his 3 showing, gets this kind of hand on Fourth Street.

You hold a pair of 10s in the hole and get:

You're now the underdog, and now it's you doing the chasing. If you had raised, how could he stay in with that garbage? No way. But you allowed him his free card and now it's a catastrophe for you. If he's shrewd, he checks, you bet, he calls. Then on Fifth Street, if you both draw blanks, he checks again, you bet to drive him out, and he hits you with a raise. Suddenly it's costing you a lot of money, and you're an underdog in a pot you should have won right away on Third Street.

We can't emphasize this tactic too much. You must raise with the premium pairs and get the weak hands out, right away.

There are exceptions, of course. If you're in early or middle position and there are at least three other higher cards out against you, then you might just call.

Suppose you have a pair of 10s and are second to bet, but you're still facing a Jack, King and Ace. Here you might be reraised and so you slowplay the 10s. If you are raised, you have to make a decision. Is the raiser trying to steal the ante? If he's in late position, he might with a scare card, such as an Ace. Then you merely call. See what happens on Fourth Street.

A favorite tactic of players in late position showing a scare card is to try and steal the ante, then, if they don't, they merely check on Fourth Street. You can bet here, especially if he's gotten a blank. If you're raised, then throw your hand away, if you haven't improved. You can't afford to chase what appear to be Aces in his hand. If he merely calls, you have to figure him for a possible small pair with an Ace sidecard, or maybe a flush draw. Your tens have the lead and you must bet into him.

Also, you might face the following. You have a pair of concealed Jacks with a 7 upcard. There's an Ace and a Queen in front of you. A 4 opened, the Ace raised and now the Queen reraises. You've got to fold. The Queens represent at least a pair of Queens to reraise an Ace, and you might be third best here.

So, the rule isn't a blind one. You attempt, whenever the situation presents itself, to raise with your premium pair, but you must use discretion when you don't hold the top pair on board and there are raises or reraises that make you believe your pair is second or third best. Then you don't even call - you fold.

However, make sure that you don't play too cautiously. Others might figure you're easy to drive out on Third Street. Alter your play. Suppose you have the 10s and an Ace in late position raises. Reraise! It's still a cheap bet, and now you may call his bluff and drive him out. If he just calls here, you can figure you've got the better hand.

If you have Aces, whether in the hole or **split**, with one showing, you must raise on Third Street, no matter what your position. You want to drive out as many players as possible. Aces, as strong as they are, lose value against several other hands.

You want to get one-on-one with these cards. Suppose you're in late position, and a player opened with a 6, and a Queen raises. Reraise. You're in a steal position and the Queen might not believe you. He may reraise. Then call. You're head to head. Your deceptive call said that you didn't really have Aces, but you like the Ace anyway in case you get another one. You can check on Fourth Street if you both don't improve. The Queens won't let you get a free card and will bet. You call. Same thing on Fifth Street. Now on Sixth Street, the hands look like this, with yours first:

**Your Hand**

**Opponent's Hand**

You're high and check. He bets and now you check raise. You've finally trapped him on Sixth Street and he'll call your raise to see the River card. He won't go out at this late street even if he knows he's second best.

The Aces are great. A former world champion was heard listening to a player moaning that the last "twelve times" he had Aces in the hole, he got beaten after forcing the action and putting in expensive raises.

"I can't take these losses", he said. "What should I do next time I get these damn Aces?"

The champion stared at him as if at a dying cockroach and said very quietly, "play them the same way." And walked away.

What's good enough for a world champion is good enough for us. When you have those Aces, raise and narrow the field against you, and if you can trap someone, do it. If you have the lead and are afraid he'll check behind you, then force the action all the way.

It's best to have concealed pairs rather than a split pair. This gives you much more room to maneuver with the premium pairs.

An ideal situation would be to have a smaller premium card as your doorcard. For example, if you have Kings in the hole and a Jack showing, you're representing Jacks when you raise. Let's say a pair of Queens reraises and for deception on Third Street, you just call. Now you get a King on Fourth Street and bet. What you're representing is that you still have the Jacks, but the King is an overcard and might come in handy if it's paired.

If you're raised on Fourth Street, just call. Check on Fifth Street if you both don't improve, and wait to Sixth Street to lower the boom by check raising, especially if he makes a running open pair, and now has Queens up. Concealed premium pairs give you this leeway to practice deception.

A final note: When playing your premium pairs, they increase in value when you see at least two of the same higher premium cards on board. For example, suppose you have a pair of Queens, and there are two Kings on board. Your Queens improve in value.

## Other Pairs

By other pairs, we mean all pairs from 2s to 9s. The chances of getting a pair of deuces are the same as getting a pair of Aces; the only difference is in the value of the cards themselves.

9s can sometimes be bet as you would a premium pair. This can happen when the board shows lower ranked cards plus a pair of premium cards. For example, there is no card higher than a 9 on board except for a a couple of Jacks held by two different players. Let's assume there's also an Ace that has folded in front of you. Now your 9s can be raised as if they were a a premium pair.

With the smaller pairs, the most important consideration is the **sidecard**, the card that is the odd card. Two 6s with a deuce is a pretty worthless hand. The 6s with an Ace is a very playable hand.

I believe that more money is lost playing the small pairs on Third Street then with any other holding.

Most weak players will automatically play a small pair to the later streets in the hope of getting trips. They don't care about the betting on Third or Fourth Street. Thus, they spend their time chasing higher pairs, and sometimes, if they do make their set of small cards, they find to their dismay that they still lose to a higher three of a kind. When that happens, they take a beating, a real bad **beat**, a professional poker expression for the worst possible loss.

If you hold a small pair, and you see another card of the same rank on board on Third Street, you should dump the pair immediately. An exception might be if you hold an Ace as a sidecard, or a King that seems to be the overcard after a couple of Aces have folded. However, a small pair with a Jack or Queen can be dumped if there's another card matching the small pair on board.

There are a lot of problems holding a small pair with a bad sidecard. It makes you the chaser and the underdog, and even if you end up with two pair, they're a small two pair that can't be aggressively bet, and any other pair showing on board makes you a probable loser.

Let's assume you started with 7s and a 3, then got 7s and 3s. But on Fifth Street, a Queen high hand gets a pair of 4s on board. You're probably up against Queens over 4s, and all you're doing is contributing to someone else's pot.

When you hold a small pair, and there's a raise on Third Street, make certain that your sidecard is higher than the raising card;

otherwise fold. For example, if you have a pair of 4s and a King, and a Jack raises, you can stay in, for the King is an overcard. But if a King raised and your sidecard was a Queen, you're out of there.

Sometimes you can determine that you're up against a drawing hand such as a three flush or three straight and if you get two pair and they miss, you're a winner. But good players may still backdoor you by staying in with a flush headed by a big card and although they miss their flush, they end up with Kings up and still beat you.

They're dangerous cards to hold, these small pairs, without a big sidecard. There are many ways to lose and just a few ways to win. You want to stay in if you're getting in real cheap, but at the sign of a couple of raises, don't play them. Your chances of getting a premium pair are as good as getting small pairs. Wait for the time when you're top dog, not just a chasing underdog.

Watch carefully to see who does stay in with small pairs, even with a blank sidecard. These are the players you want in the game, for you can punish them severely.

Anytime you see the showdown, where a player reveals his hole cards to be a small pair and another small card, and he's been chasing some paint on board, you know this guy is a weakie. Wait for your moment against him. He's falling in love with any pair and that's good news for you.

### Three To A Flush

This is a pure drawing hand, but it may turn into a different sort of hand if a card or two pairs. The most important criterion to this kind of hand is the card that's heading it. A three to a flush with an Ace is very strong, for you may miss the flush and still get Aces up. Also, if you're up against another flush, an Ace high flush is the strongest.

If your three to a flush consists of three small cards, they're playable if you don't have to call two raises on Third Street. One raise keeps you in. With three clubs, for example, an 8 5 and 3, you really don't have any outs.

So two reraises at the outset on Third Street, and you're gone. Otherwise it's going to be a long expensive process and you're a **dog** all the way. You're not the favorite to win.

Another consideration is the number of cards of that suit out against you on Third Street. You can only see what is in your hand and on the board. If there are three cards of the same suit on the board, throw your hand away. The odds have gotten scrunched, and there's no reason to go for the flush.

But if there are two or fewer cards out, there's only been one raise, and your three flush is headed by a premium card, you can stay in the pot, hoping to draw out or get in by the **backdoor**. By that, we mean win the hand in a way you didn't expect to win it. For example, you start off with King, 10 and 8 of diamonds and end up with Kings over 8s and win the pot.

With three small cards to a flush, the chances of winning by the backdoor become very slight. The ideal situation for you to is to limp in on Third Street, without a raise against you. Or one raise at the most.

With drawing hands you want to conserve as much money as possible, until you become the favorite or form the drawing hand.

For example, suppose you hold Ace, 10 and 5 of hearts. A King has raised on Third Street and a Queen and 9 have called. You call also.

On Fourth Street, you get a fourth heart, the 7. Now you are the favorite in this hand. You've got an overcard above the King, and you've gotten four hearts by Fourth Street. And there is multi-pot action. You can raise in this situation.

If you didn't get the fourth heart, and two hearts come out, and you didn't pair, you should throw away the hand on Fourth Street. Let's say that not only did two hearts come out, in addition to two on Third Street, but an Ace came out as well. Your chances for a win here have narrowed considerably. You've got to pray for a fourth and then a fifth heart or an Ace, and the odds have sunk for these draws. Dump the cards.

To summarize, three to a flush is a playable hand, but not if three cards of that suit are out on Third Street. The higher the top card, the stronger is the three suit. With three weak cards to a flush, go out against two raises on Third Street.

## Three to a Straight

This is a weaker hand than three to a flush, but the same principles pretty well apply. The higher the straight potential, the easier to play. For example, three to a low straight may be a marginal hand unless you can limp in without a raise.

Suppose you hold the following:

This is a borderline hand at best. Unless you draw and make the straight, you probably have a losing hand. Pairing any of the cards doesn't really improve your hand that much. For instance, if you get a 6 of clubs on Fourth Street, all you now have is a small pair with a weak overcard, the 8. If any sort of rag comes up on Fifth Street, you've got to throw away this hand.

If you can limp in with a weak three to a straight, fine. If you're raised by a player who you think is trying to steal the pot in a late position, you can stay in with a small three to a straight. However, an early raise should give you pause. Why play the hand as an underdog, a hand you'll probably have to stay with to the river? If there are two raises, you're definitely out of there on Third Street.

The minimum hand you want to play with a three straight, absorbing a raise, is a hand containing some paint. For example, a three card holding of 10, Jack and Queen is a good drawing hand with a number of outs.

You can stay in against two raises to Fourth Street, but if there's no improvement on that Street, then fold them up.

For example, your Fourth Street holding looks like this:

You see a King on board as well as an 8. The King raised on Third Street and comes out betting, the 8 calls. Why are you in? If you pair the Queen or Jack, you're still chasing a pair of Kings in all probability.

If you're holding a 2, 3, 4, unsuited, these are cards most pros will throw away automatically, even if they can limp in. There are absolutely no outs here. They can be beaten by all kinds of hands. I would dump them as well, not even seeing Fourth Street.

On the other hand, a holding of Jack, Queen, King, unsuited, is your best possible three to a straight, even better than Queen, King, Ace, as far as drawing possibilities exist. You have an open ended straight rather than having one end closed up by the Ace.

With this hand you have a number of outs. If a Jack or Queen has raised on Third Street, you still have an overcard with the King. This hand is not only a drawing hand for a high straight, but a hand where a high pair can easily form.

Hands with two to a flush are slightly stronger than hands with three cards unsuited, because there is the backdoor possibility, however slight, that you can form a flush with your hand. For example, the first hand is stronger than the one that follows it:

**First Hand**

**Second Hand**

Sometimes a hand can move in both directions. For example,

the first hand may now look like this on Sixth Street.

Now you have both a flush and straight draw. But you still have a drawing hand as the River card is about to be dealt, and unless you form a straight or flush you're probably going to pay off somebody.

Another concept to look at with a three to a straight hand is the number of players in at Third Street. Unless you have a hand headed by at least a Queen, you don't want to be in against only one other player. You're better off throwing away the hand.

If the other player has raised from an early position with a King, despite an Ace being behind him, he may hold a pair of Kings and this two way action means you'll be chasing him to the River. Perhaps he doesn't hold Kings. Maybe he has a three flush headed by a King. In any event, what are you doing in there against him? He has the lead and you've got to chase with your Queen high three straight.

When going for a straight, you want at least three way action on Third Street, to build up a pot. Otherwise most threes to a straight aren't playable.

To summarize, the higher the Three straight, the stronger it is. Throw away small Three Straights unless you can limp in and if you don't improve the straight on Fourth Street, throw your hand away. Don't play a three to a straight against two raises. Don't stay in without an overcard in two way action.

## Other Playable Hands

The bigger the game, and the higher the ante structure, the more hands you're going to play. You have to; otherwise the antes will eat you up. You've got to fight for them. And you can be assured other players are also playing weaker hands, so it's a push there.

However, you don't want to play hands so weak you can't win with them unless you get miracle cards. You still want to have a chance. And the weaker the ante structure, the more you're going to tighten up your game.

Games like $5-$10, $10-$20 and even $15-$30 are going to call for much tighter playing hands. In the first two levels, there's absolutely no reason to play borderline hands. Stick with all the categories we mentioned, period.

The one exception is limping in with three premium cards, or two premium cards headed by an Ace. Thus, if you're dealt the following:

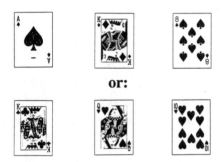

or:

You have playable hands. If you can limp in with them, fine. If you have to take a raise from a player who you think is trying to steal the ante, fine. If the big cards are hidden in the hole, even better.

However, other factors enter into the picture. If with Ace-King in the hole, an Ace has raised at Third Street, what's the use in playing? If he has Aces, you have a pretty dead hand. And it's going to cost you to find out. Suppose he had a Queen instead and raised with it?

With this situation, you still want to play Fourth Street. Now, if you get paired, you're in business. For example, with your Ace, King in the hole and 8 on board, facing a Queen that raised, you get an Ace or King, you've got the lead.

The beauty of holding high cards, even though they're unmatched is the possibility of pairing one of them by Fifth Street, when the second tier of betting kicks in. If no improvement, dump them.

With these hands, as with all hands, having two to a flush makes the hands that wee bit stronger. There's another out, the distant possibility of a flush forming.

But remember, with a high ante structure, you may be playing these hands more often. Often it depends on the style of other players. If a player is super aggressive and is trying to roll over everyone, you've got to stand up with your Ace, King in the hole. If, on the other hand, a player is tight, you might throw them away.

Most players will always play an Ace, King, Queen, but this isn't the greatest hand in the world. It loses quite often. Unless you pair by Fifth Street, you will probably get beaten with it. Don't fall in love with the hand, and if there are two raises on Third Street, I'd get rid of this hand. I'd much rather have a small pair with an Ace or King as sidecard, than an Ace, King, Queen.

Broken straights are tempting hands, but they're generally losers. For example, you have 8 diamonds, 9 spades, Jack of clubs. If you don't get the 10 or pair the Jack, what do you really have, but garbage? Unless you have outs, such as a hand holding King of diamonds, Queen of clubs and a 10 of diamonds, you don't want to play these split and broken straights. They look tempting, and in a rare instance you'll go out and see the card you wanted fall where your hand should have been. But even if that's the case, what do you really have but a four straight at this point?

Two to a flush is a better hand than unsuited cards, but you don't want to play it unless it's headed by strong paint, such as a King or Ace. Maybe a Queen, if a Jack has raised on Third Street. If the Ace or King is your doorcard, you might raise to steal the ante. If called, you aren't in the best of shape. If reraised, throw your cards away. But again, with a high ante structure, knowing your opponents' styles will give you an insight into what move you should make.

We can't emphasize in strong enough language that you must be alert at the poker table, and study your opponents, even when you're out of the individual game. See how they play. Watch to see what they turn over at the showdown, or what hands they concede to. You know how to play your cards; the important thing is to put them on a hand correctly. If you can't do this, you're going to have trouble winning, unless you get a series of strong winning hands.

You can't depend on luck in poker; it's the skill that separates the men from the boys.

**Garbage Hands**

Don't even think of playing them. If you have a scare card, you might try a raise on Third Street to force out other players and try to steal the ante, or hope to pair the scare card or get another one to win, outright on Fourth Street.

But there's really no other reason to play garbage hands without pairs or real drawing possibilities. It just costs money. Even if you've been getting a run of terrible unplayable hands, keep throwing them away. Be patient. One of the awards of patience is saving money.

Above all, don't try and bluff with junk. It gets you nowhere. With skill you should have moves to make at the table, as this book shows, but you don't want pure bluffs that will be called and cost you money. The more skill you have, the fewer your bluffs.

On the other hand, if your opponents play garbage, punish them. If they are hoping lightning will strike their cards with miracle draws, make them pay for their foolishness. Some players lose their patience and play garbage. Others may be drunk and fall in love with all kinds of cards. In any event, these are the kinds of opponents you want. But don't you fall into the same trap.

**Fourth Street**

Fourth Street can be a key round of play. This is **the turn**, as poker players call it, and now you'll be able to get a better feel of the opponents' hands, since two cards are in the open.

Let us analyze various hands and see what to do on Fourth Street.

**Trips**

Having trips on Third Street, if you get a Four of a Kind hand now, the best move is to check if you're first to bet.

Suppose you started with deuces rolled up, and now get a fourth deuce. The best thing to do is check them, if you're first. If someone else bets and there's a raise, simply call the raise. What you're now representing is that you stayed in with your deuce because you might have three to a flush or another pair, and now you might have two pair, with the second pair not too big since you didn't reraise the raiser when the bet came back to you on Third Street.

More likely, you'll get an odd card to go with your rolled up trips. If another hand is high on board and bets, call here. If there's a raise after you, call the raise. It isn't time yet to raise with your hand. You have to be patient, build the pot up, so that, when you do start raising there'll be an element of deception, since you'll raise on a card that doesn't seem to help your hand.

Let's assume that you started with a pair and now get trips on Fourth Street. The main factor here is whether you paired your door card to get the trips or you make the set based on two hole cards. Suppose you now hold:

An Ace bets and a Queen calls. You might raise right here, because you're representing not trips but a four flush with at least a King heading it. By raising, you're disguising your hand sufficiently. It would even be a better raise if there are a few hearts out already. The Ace might come back at you, and then you call.

If you pair your doorcard, you have a different situation. Professional poker players have calculated that a player pairing a door card is a favorite to have trips immediately if no other card of the same rank has shown, and a dog to have trips if there's another card of the same rank out.

Let's assume that your hand is:

You're high on board. You have an option of betting the lower or the higher tier of the game. Let's assume it's $15-$30. You can bet either $15 or $30. Or of course, you can check.

The best move is to bet $30. It's almost an automatic bet. If you bet $15, it might be more scarier for the other players. They'll figure you for trips, and you're trying to suck them in. If you only have 9s, why not just check. You see a lot of this lower tiered bet in the smaller games against unsophisticated players.

The $30 bet doesn't reveal anything about the value of your hand. Most players will bet with an open pair when they have the lead, and that's all you're doing. Now a player holding the Ace thinks he's sharp and wants to test to see whether you have trips, so he raises. He holds:

You simply call. Let him think you don't have the trips. The other hand is now:

He calls. You've got to figure him for Queens here. Maybe three clubs. You don't mind having him in. You want as many players in as possible and you figure to win without even improving. On Fifth Street the hands look like this:

**Yours:**

67

**Opponents:**

Now we have a choice to make. The concept of the free card comes in here. As you may recall, a free card is a situation where a player bets or raises the round before in order to get himself a free card, that is, a free round of play where no bets are made.

If you check here, and the Ace and Queen hands check, you've given free cards to two players, and if they now beat you by drawing a great card on Sixth Street, you've made a really bad play.

If you do check, the only purpose is to check raise. Betting out may not give away too much of your hand. If you have two pair now, it looks as if neither card your opponents got helped them. So you bet. The Ace raises, the Queen hesitates and calls the raise, and now you reraise.

Both hands have put in too much money for them to now go out. You're up against Aces up in one situation, and maybe Queens up or a four-straight (unlikely) in the other situation. You get two calls for your reraise.

On Sixth Street, the hands look like this:

**Yours:**

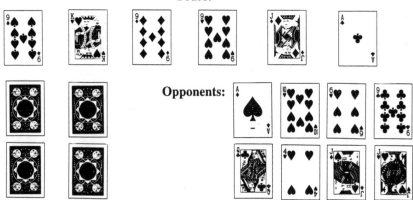

68

The Jacks are high and bet out. You raise, figuring that this is merely a second pair. You already have a Jack. Also, the buying of an Ace by you defused the strength of the Ace high hand. His drawing of your fourth 9 is ok for you, since there's no way it can help him. It's just a dead card in his hand. After you raise, both the Ace and the pair of Jacks call.

On Seventh Street, you either get the second pair or don't. If the Jacks bet out, you figure to lose against a higher trips or possibly a full house. If they check, you can bet here. You're probably facing Queens up and Aces or Aces up. You get two calls and should win the pot with your trips.

**Pairing the Doorcard**

This will call for an almost automatic bet if you're in the lead, unless you've gotten a miracle card to give you four of a kind. Then you check and slowplay the hand. What if you pair the doorcard and a player with a bigger doorcard pairs his? If there's no other card out of his ranked doorcards, you have to think that he has a set now. If you don't have a set, but merely two pair or less, with your other pair less than the paired doorcard of your opponent, you can pack away the cards and fold them.

For example you hold:

Your opponent:

On Third Street, he had raised with the Jacks before you, and you merely called. Now, you've got to figure he has a set of Jacks. Of course, he might not, but you still might be chasing him all the way. If he has, or gets a second pair, he has you beat anyway. Fold your two pair here.

A lot of players who come from home games don't understand the concept of the paired doorcard and don't really respect its strength. That's because their home games are looser and the players they're up against go in with all kinds of borderline hands, so the pairing of a doorcard means that the opponent has a pair, nothing more.

But in the tighter confines of casino poker, where players throw away a lot more hands than they do in home games, a paired doorcard means trouble for you. It's not always the case, but most times, if no other card of the same rank is out, the player already has a set. If you see another card of the same rank out, or if you have one in the hole, you figure he doesn't have trips. The odds are against it, but he might still have the set.

A lot of players immediately raise against paired doorcards, testing whether or not the player has a set. But that may be a bad move. A strong player may not reraise if he has trips, and if he doesn't have the trips but reraises anyway then he forces the raiser to throw his cards away. It's a bad move against sophisticated players. Against weak players it might work, for they'll reraise with trips and just call without them. Then you can play your hand accordingly.

On Fourth Street, if you feel you have the highest holding, it's always important to make sure there's betting on this Street. For example, if you have a pair of Queens, but your board shows Queen - 10, and an Ace checks, get in a bet. If you don't bet, that Ace, and any other hand will probably get a free card, which is something a leader never wants to give up. In essence, you're allowing inferior hands another card to improve, without making a bet. A bad play!

In fact, I always feel it's a good move to bet when high hand on board checks to you. If you don't have a decent hand, you shouldn't be in the pot anyway. Even if you have a drawing hand, but with a scarecard showing, a bet might win the pot for you right then and there. If nothing else, it might give you a free card on

Fifth Street, the more expensive street.

Sometimes a raise is in order to get that free card yourself on Fifth Street, especially if you have a pure drawing hand. For example, suppose you hold:

Your opponent, who has the lead, holds:

He bets, and you raise. You discount the Ace, because you have one also, and count on him holding a pair, possibly Queens. Or he may hold a pair of 8s with a high kicker. Or he may have a three straight or three flush and the Ace didn't help at all, but it's a scare card and he bets accordingly.

Now, if he calls your raise and he doesn't improve on Fifth Street, he'll probably check to you. You've gotten a free card. Never underestimate that free card, for, in essence, it gives you two cards to look at without putting in a bet. You not only get Fifth Street, but Sixth Street as well, before you have to make a decision. If your drawing hand has gone nowhere, you can throw your cards away at Sixth Street when your opponent bets.

To get that free card, you put in an extra bet on Fourth Street and make sure you don't have the lead on Fifth Street. Thus, the opponent must have a higher board than you have. Of course you may pair on Fifth Street and have the lead, but that's okay. You can bet now, and force the opponent to throw away his cards.

Most of the time on Fourth Street, you won't improve your hand, but will have to wait till the later streets to see what happens. That doesn't mean that you don't bet anyway. You want to force the action if you feel you have the best hand so far, get more money into that pot. You don't want to give away a free card. And

71

you're always looking for a free card on Fifth Street if you hold an inferior hand, or a pure drawing hand.

If you're going for a straight or flush, and you don't improve the hand on Fourth Street, you should consider folding if you have to take a raise on that Street. If any opponent pairs his doorcard, you're definitely out. In our previous example, the 10 of spades now gave us a three flush and a three to a straight, so it was an improvement. But if our opponent had paired his doorcard, we're outta there.

If you get the fourth card to a suit or to the straight on Fourth Street, you're going to go all the way to the River with that hand. So you have to be prepared to take raises and still stay in. Again, the best situation would be to maneuver for that free card on Fifth Street, to get at least one free card.

If you hold a three to a flush or three to a straight and don't improve on Fourth Street, and you have no overcard, it's time to throw away the hand. You have no outs here. If you have an overcard (a higher card than is on the board) you might stay for one raise, but throw your cards away rather than going for a double raise.

With three high cards, such as Ace hearts, Queen diamonds, Jack clubs, or even if two are suited, if you don't improve the hand on Fourth Street, throw them away. The only exception here would be getting a third to a suit or pairing one of the high cards. Otherwise you're gone.

## Fifth Street

On Fifth Street, we're in the higher tier of betting, and it and subsequent streets become expensive. We're now striving to win the pot with our cards. We don't just want to make a fine showing, coming in second or third, because there's no payoff for place or show, just for winning. And one of the most expensive ways to lose money in poker is to constantly have second-best hand.

If we have four to a flush or four to a straight, we are going to the River, no matter what card we get on Fifth Street. If we previously had only three to a flush or three to a straight and now got our fourth formed card, we're still going to the River.

If we haven't improved our three to a straight or three to a flush, we throw away the cards here.

If we hold a pair, and it's obvious that an opponent has a higher pair, either by pairing on board, or by the way he's been betting, we dump our cards. If we pair on board, or make our second pair, we're in betting and raising if no one else has improved on board. That's why the concept of going in with a pair with a big sidecard is so important. It enables us to have top hand here, rather than holding two inferior pairs.

If we get trips on Fifth Street, we should be patient and not raise on this Street.

For example, suppose our hand is:

We face two opponents. One opponent shows:

And the other:

The Queen of spades opens, the Jack of diamonds calls, and now it's up to us. If we raise, they'll probably call and then check to us on Sixth Street, giving us no room to deceive or maneuver.

So we call. We figure we're looking at Queens and probably deuces with an Ace kicker.

On Sixth Street, here's the situation:

73

**Our hand:**

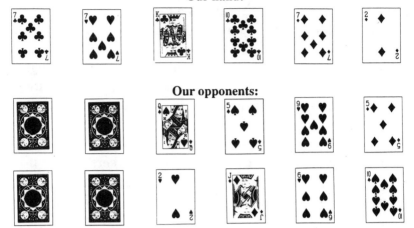

**Our opponents:**

The 5s bet, the other hand goes out, and now we raise.

The holder of the fives looks over our cards and thinks "what does he have?" Good question. It's difficult to read our hand. Maybe Kings up. So he calls, and checks on Sixth Street and then calls our bet there.

Thus, one of the tenets of Fifth Street play is to be patient. If we feel we have the top hand, we want to wait till Sixth Street, if someone else is leading the betting, to get our raises in.

This adds to the deception of our hand and makes it harder to figure out, and it enables us to get in some extra bets. By Sixth Street, the opponent is going to call our raise. He has a lot in the pot, the pot is big and he wants to see the River card.

**Sixth Street**

If we have a disguised hand, this is where we generally make our move and raise if another player opens. If we're reraised, we have to decide whether to call or put in one more raise. Generally speaking, if our hand isn't yet formed, we might just call. Thus, with trips we'd call, but if we already have the full house, we go ahead and reraise.

Sixth Street is pretty simple to play otherwise. By Fifth Street, we've dumped our drawing hands that haven't improved. We're now in with four to a straight or four to a flush if we haven't formed a complete hand and we want to stay in as cheaply as possible.

If we feel we have the top hand, we want to get as many raises in as possible. If the opponent's board is full of blanks (cards that don't seem to help him) we will lead the action with a pair of Aces, or another high pair if we feel we have top pair.

For example:

**Our hand:**

**Opponent:**

We can bet out here. Previously we had the lead and were called. We have to figure him for Queens, not Aces, for with Aces, he would have reraised even on Third Street. But that's not been the case.

If we're up against a drawing hand, figuring that the opponent has four to a flush or four to a straight, we bet out our hand. We want him to pay for the privilege of seeing that last card. No free rides here.

The idea is not to check if you're in the lead. If the high hand checks to you, throw in a bet. That will also improve your table image, for players will realize that they've got to pay if they stay in with you. It'll make them throw away some hands that might have hurt you.

## Seventh Street

Now we're at the River, at the end of the line. No more cards to buy, no way to improve our hand. A great champion who I interviewed had this philosophy about Seventh Street.

"Always bet out. This gives you two ways to win. First, if you're called, you might have the best hand. Secondly, you might not be called. Either way you win. The only way to lose is if he has better cards." Or, I might add, he raises you, forcing you to put in another bet, and then you lose the pot.

Sometimes this is going to happen, when the board of the opponent seems filled with garbage, rags and blanks.

Those three hole cards can give him a powerful hidden hand, such as a flush or straight (if two cards are on the board to the flush or straight), trips, and of course a full house. He can even have a Four of a Kind hand, but we don't consider that unless you have an obvious high full house, such as three Aces on board and he raises you after you bet.

However, in playing poker, you can't always fear the **nuts**, the situation where an opposing player has the absolutely best hand. That's not always going to happen. You should be able to get a good read from the board and the way he's already played his hand. You should have observed him and gotten a feel of the style of his game. All these factors have to be equated before your betting decision on Seventh Street.

I recall playing against a *rock* in a $10-$20 game. If he had the best hand, he'd raise, and if he had a trailing hand, he'd just call. On Sixth Street, I had three 9s, two of them in the hole, and bet. He raised. His board looked like this:

Up to then he had merely called. I put him on a heart flush, so I called his raise. On Seventh Street, I made another pair, giving me a full house. Since he was a rock, I knew he'd just call if I bet, fearing that I made my hand. But if I checked, he wouldn't allow me off the hook. So I checked, he bet and I raised. He just called, and conceded his hand to my full house. I got in an extra bet that way.

If you're up against a player with a drawing hand, who's showing three or four to a flush or straight, but hasn't made it yet on Sixth Street, the best move is to check on the River if you hold the potential winning hand, but not one that beats a flush or straight. For instance, if you hold trips or two pair, and haven't improved on the River, the safest play is to check.

If he doesn't make his hand, he'll check also and your hand will win. If he bets, you just put in one bet. He may be bluffing. However, if you bet and he raised, it's a tougher call. If he's made his hand he'll raise and if he hasn't he'll check behind you. There's no reason to bet out and hope he didn't make his hand. You'll end up either making an extra bet or throwing your cards away, wondering if you've been bluffed.

Often a player on Seventh Street will say "check in the blind," as he shuffles his cards around without looking at his new River card. I usually bet outright when that happens; because good players don't do this. They make a decision after looking at their River card. Usually, but not always, of course, a player who says "check in the blind," has a weak hand and is praying that you won't bet out so he has to call another bet. He's also afraid of being bluffed, and will usually call your bet, not raise it.

Another weakness you can detect in players is the statement, "check to the raiser." This can come on any Street. When I hear this I usually make an automatic bet. Only amateurs and losers use that statement. A better player will simply check if he has the lead. Of course he's checking to the raiser, if you've raised the round before. Why repeat the obvious? But those two remarks make me think I'm facing weak players. "Check in the blind." "Check to the raiser."

What about bluffing on Seventh Street? It's tough to do, unless a player traps himself with an inopportune bet and suddenly faces two raises, yours the last of the two. Usually, by Seventh Street, there's a big pot out there, the bets are limited on the River, and an astute player wants to see what you have for the price of just another bet.

It's easier to bluff a strong player, than it is to bluff a weak player, however. A strong player will weigh your moves from Third Street, study the board and your betting patterns, and if he feels he's beaten, he'll give up the hand on occasion. The weak player is fearful of being bluffed, as though this reflects on his manhood, and with any sort of hand, a pair of 3s, will call a board that has a King, Jack and Queen on it.

A rock is not going to try and bluff you, but a strong player in correct position behind you may put in a raise with that intention. You must now study the situation and reflect back on his cards and his bets on the cards and try to make an intelligent decision. Or simply call the raise. One more bet is better than forfeiting the entire pot to an inferior hand.

# VII. TEXAS HOLD 'EM

**Introduction**

In the last decade, this poker game has grown in popularity to the point where it has overtaken 7-Stud as the most popular of the casino poker games. This is especially true in many of the California poker clubs, where the game is played with stakes ranging from $1-$2 all the way up to $300-$600 in clubs like the Bicycle Club in Bell Gardens.

Those who are experts at the game claim it is the most complex of poker games. There are five community cards in Hold 'em, all on board and all seen by all the players.

Thus the complexity. If you hold a good hand, so may your opponents. And you can use both of your pocket cards originally dealt to you, or one of them, or simply use the board without making use of any pocket card to create your best hand.

Many players like the game because it is more relaxing than 7-Stud. The only thing you have to concentrate on are the players' actions and the board, whereas in 7-Stud you must follow each player's cards as they are dealt on the various Streets.

This is not the case in Hold 'em. The board is dealt to the middle of the table, clearly visible to all players, and the players at either end of the table don't have to lean forward to see what the players' hands at the other end look like.

It is also a good action game. Whereas a player in 7-Stud needs only 40 times the minimum bet to stay comfortably in the game, in Hold 'em, it's more like 100 times the minimum bet. There's more betting, more action, more raises and reraises. Thus there's more money to be won, or if one has bad luck to lose.

## How the Game is Played

Hold 'em is more popular as a casino than as a private game. In private games, players generally play looser games often with additional cards bought to turn a 7-Stud game into one where nine cards are seen by all players.

Hold 'em, while a looser game generally, is best played in a casino setting, where 9 players sit at a table, a situation difficult in a private game. Also, despite more betting in Hold 'em, it's not a game that accommodates itself to extra buying of cards. It has a rigid structure, unlike 7-Stud in private homes, where players often have the option of buying two additional cards to strengthen their hands.

Also, 7-Stud can be played as a high-low game, where both the high hand and the low hand share the pot. This isn't the case in Hold 'em. It's strictly a High poker game.

A variant of Hold 'em is Omaha Eight or Better, which is played as a high-low game. The difficulty in playing regular Hold 'em as a high-low game is the scarcity of cards the player sees. He only gets two pocket cards and five on the board. That's it.

In a casino, a dealer handles the cards, shuffles and cuts them and then deals them out. Since position is of importance in Hold 'em, a button is passed around the table, going from one player to another in a clockwise direction. The one **on the button** is the theoretical dealer, and gets his cards last and bets last on the first and every subsequent round of play.

Since all the board cards are community cards, there's no high hand *per se*. The button's place on the table determines where the betting starts and stops.

In the Vegas casinos there's no ante involved with Hold 'em. The player to the left of the button, and the player to this player's left, must both put in bets prior to the cards being dealt. These are called **blinds**. Generally speaking, the first blind is half the size of the second, and the second blind equals the minimum bet allowed.

For example, if the game is $10-$20, the first blind is $5, and the second blind is $10. Those bets are out on the table before any cards are dealt, and are mandatory.

In the California clubs, there is usually an ante, plus a single blind. In those clubs the blind is equal to the minimum bet. However, each club has different rules. In some clubs there's two blinds plus an ante.

But no matter where you play, in Vegas or California or at home, if there is a blind, it's a **live blind.** This means that after everyone bets, the blinds have the option of raising when the bets get back to them.

## The Deal and the Streets

After the blind bets are made, the dealer deals out one card at a time, face down to each player at the table, beginning with the player to the left of the button, going clockwise. Thus the button gets the last card dealt in each round of dealing, till everyone has two cards face down.

After this aspect of the deal, each player has what are known as his **pocket cards.** A round of betting follows. The first one to act is the player to the left of the last blind bet. He must match that bet or can raise it. Or he can fold. There's no checking permitted on this round of betting.

When the betting gets back to the blinds, they can also raise or simply call the last bet.

Let's say that three players have called the **big blind** (the second or larger of the blinds) and now it's up the **small blind** (the smaller of the blinds) to match the bet. In a typical $10-$20 game, the small blind put in $5 and the big blind, betting after him, had to bet $10.

Since three players called the $10 bet, the small blind, to stay in play, would have to bet an additional $5. Or he could raise. Or he could fold, leaving his $5 in the pot as dead money. Let's say he decides to fold, but the Big Blind decides to raise the bet to $20.

This is what action looks like at this point.

| | |
|---|---|
| **Small Blind**: | $5 |
| **Big Blind**: | $10 |
| **Third Player**: | Folds |
| **Fourth Players**: | Folds |
| **Fifth Players**: | $10 |
| **Sixth Players**: | $10 |
| **Seventh Player**: | $10 |
| **Eighth Player**: | Folds |
| **Ninth Players**: | Folds |
| **Small Blind**: | Folds |
| **Big Blind**: | Raises to $20 |

Now all those remaining in the game, the Fifth, Sixth and Seventh Players, must match the raise, reraise or fold. If there is reraising, only three raises are allowed on any one round, unless there are only two players remaining in the game, in which case raises can be unlimited.

If the Big Blind didn't want to raise, all he'd do when it was his turn to bet again would be to indicate to the dealer by gesture or by voice, that he didn't intend to raise.

Now, after all bets have been made, the dealer **burns** a card (takes the top card and slides it out of play) and deals out three cards face up. This is called the **flop**. These are all community cards, and any player can make use of at least one or all three if it improves his hand.

This is what a board might look like:

Now another round of betting ensues.

Again, the player closest to the button's left bets first. This is the Big Blind. Now he can check and come into the betting later.

Check raising is also permitted. After he bets, assuming he bets, then all the other players remaining must either match the bet, raise or match a raise or fold. Bets on the flop are still in the lower tier of betting. Thus, in our game, it would still be at the $10 level.

Now, after all bets are in, the dealer burns another card and deals one more card. This is Fourth Street. The board might look like this:

Again, the betting is in the same sequence. After this round of betting, in $20 bets and raises, there is the final card dealt on board. This is the River, Fifth Street. The board is complete and looks like this:

A final round of betting occurs on Fifth Street, in the same order as the other Streets. After all bets are made, there is a show-down. The person called shows his cards first and the others may show their cards if they have a better hand, or concede.

Sometimes, because of the complexity of the possible winning hands, a player may show his hand in case he has a winning hand, or has a **push**, a tie.

Let's assume that only two players remain for the showdown and one holds 6 diamonds, Queen diamonds.

Another player, the one called, held 6 hearts, Jack hearts.

Neither player wins the entire pot. The best hand here is 6s and 5s, two pair with the King kicker. Since neither player holds a card higher than a King as a side card, it's a tie and the pot is split. If one of the two held 6, Ace, he'd be the winner. The winning hand would then be a pair of 6s and a pair of 5s with the Ace kicker.

Note that, in the two hands we previously showed, each player only used one of his pocket cards, the 6, to establish his best hand. Each used the pair of 5s, the 6 and the King from the board to establish his best five-card hand.

### Reading the Flop

Hold 'em, as we mentioned, is a complicated game, with the board yielding all sorts of possibilities. One of the more pleasant factors about the game is that a player can find himself with the absolute "nuts," the very best unbeatable hand. It happens quite a bit in Hold 'em, and rarely in a game like 7-Stud. Here's an example of this:

**The player holds:**

**The Board:**

The best hand here is an Ace high flush, and no other player can possibly have a better hand. If you hold the Ace 7 of hearts, you have an absolute lock on the win. The pot is yours.

That is a consideration in Hold 'em, whether you have a chance at the nuts, or whether another player has a chance. This is a distinct possibility because only two cards are hidden. If there are no pairs on the board, and only two to a flush or a straight, then no one can make a straight or flush or full house. So sometimes you can have the nuts with a comparatively weak hand:

Let's say you hold:

The board is:

There is no way to make a flush or straight with this board. There is no card higher than a Queen on board, so even if another player had Kings or Aces, he wouldn't improve his hand. Your three Queens are the nuts.

However, this is a rare board. Usually, there is some outside chance that a player can get a strong hand from the board if he's holding the right cards. Let's look at this board:

If a player holds a 6, 7 he can make a straight here. Since there are no pairs on board, there is no chance of a full house beating him. And no one can make a flush against him.

So, you must be aware of the complicated holdings that can develop from your pocket cards and the five cards on the board. And also remember, if you're developing a good hand from the board, so may another player, who can beat you.

Suppose you hold:

The board:

You can hold Aces up, with a Queen kicker. You can be beaten

85

if any player holds a trey in his hand, for he should have at least trips. It is unlikely, you feel, and even if you're right, you can still lose to an Ace, Jack which would give an opponent Aces over Jacks. Or a player can hold Ace, King, and beat you with the odd card.

So, while there's the factor of the nuts helping you, there's the other factor of a multitude of hands that can beat you, even if you have comparatively strong hands.

## BEFORE THE FLOP
### The Pocket Cards - What to Hold

What cards you hold to play with, and what cards you discard and won't bet on, is the most important aspect of your strategy in Hold 'em. If you keep holding bad, garbage cards, occasionally you'll make a miraculous win, but more often than not, it'll cost you a ton of money. You must be selective in what you bet on. Let's run down the possible cards to stay with.

Of course, if you're the big blind and haven't been raised before the flop, you'll stay on anything. You've been forced in. But other than that situation you must be discriminating.

### Position

Before we deal with the cards you should hold at the outset of play, we must discuss position, which is of vital importance in Hold 'em. Most of the time, your position at the table will determine the strategy you follow. The later the position, the better your relative situation at the table.

In the worst position are the blinds, the small and big blind. They not only act first, but they've committed money to the pot already. Since both blinds are *live*, that is, they can raise when the betting get around to them again, they are not completely impotent.

If there are some callers with no raises, it is not automatic for the small blind to bet the extra $5 to see the flop. If he has terrible cards, he's merely throwing more good money after bad. And he is still not the last player to act. The Big Blind can still raise.

However, in the Big Blind's position, if there are no raises and the bet gets back to him, he can stay with any cards dealt, such as a 7 2 offsuit, or a 3 2 offsuit. He has nothing to lose. He's getting a free look at the Flop.

Let's assume a ten-handed game in a Vegas casino to define position. We know the blinds have been forced to put in money in the pot. The three positions to the Big Blind's left can be called **early position.**

In early position, you need stronger cards than you do in middle or later position to enter the betting. In **middle position**, which is the next three players after the three early position players, we need somewhat weaker cards to get involved in the action. Finally, the last two players are in the ideal **late position**, with the button the very best, and need the weakest of all cards, plus they can make the most moves.

An important consideration is that the relative position of the player doesn't change from the first two cards dealt to Seventh Street. Knowing what relative position is at the Hold 'em table, let's examine the first two cards dealt, the pocket cards.

## Premium Cards

The very best cards you can be dealt at the outset we'll call **premium cards**. These cards can be played from any position, and you must see the flop with them, no matter how many raises you have to absorb. Let's see them in order.

- •Ace-Ace
- •King-King
- •Ace-King suited
- •Queen-Queen
- •Jack-Jack

You should also be prepared to raise with these cards in any position. With hands like Aces or Kings, or Ace-King suited, you can reraise a raiser. They're that strong. With Queens and Jacks, they can be raised in middle or late position, if there have been no raises before your bet.

## Other Playable Hands- Strong
- Ace-Queen • Ace-Jack • Ace-10 • all suited
- Ace-King
- King-Queen suited
- 10-10
- King-Jack • Queen-Jack • Jack-10 • all suited
- Ace-Queen • Ace-Jack
- 9-9
- King-Queen
- King-10 suited • Queen-10 suited

## Playable Hands - Somewhat Strong
- 8-8
- Jack-9 • 10-9 • both suited
- 7-7
- 9-8 • 8-7 • both suited
- Ace with any other suited card
- King-Jack • Queen-Jack • Jack-10

## Playable Hands - Mediocre
- Any pair below 7s
- Connected suited cards, such as:7-6, 6-5, 5-4, 4-3
- Ace-10 • King-10 • Queen-10
- King-9 • Jack-8 • both suited

## Weaker Hands
- All other cards.

## Strategy Before the Flop

This list is not to be taken as a rigid listing of hands from top to bottom in terms of strength. Whether a pair of 7s is stronger than a 9-8 suited may be problematical. What the list of hands shows is what hands we consider playable in terms of relative strength.

As a general rule, you'll raise with the Premium Hands no matter what position you're in, with the exception of Queens and

Jacks, which are best raised in middle or late position, if no one has raised before you. With the Aces, Kings and Ace King suited, you can reraise any raise, no matter what position you're in.

With the Strong Playable hands you are looking to raise with these cards in middle or late position if no one has raised in front of you. If there are a couple of calls only, your raise is more effective. If everyone before you has folded, you can raise even with the Somewhat Strong hands.

What you don't want to allow is some mediocre hand to stay in and possibly buy a miracle board. Also, you don't want to be tagged as a rock, a player who raises only with the very best cards. Terrific deceptive cards in this regard are the medium connected cards, such as 9 spades - 8 spades. Suppose you raise, and the flop comes up:

If it's checked to you, you come out betting, with most players putting you on Kings. Now, if Fourth Street is perfect, with a 5, you have a very deceptive hand.

If the River looks like this:

You may get some action from Aces up or another two-pair hand, and it's difficult to figure you for the straight. Or someone else may have the **ignorant end** (or lower end) of the straight, staying in with 4-3.

If you're the button, and thus in last position, if there have been no raises before you, you can call with weaker hands than if you were in the first position. With any kind of possibilities, for instance, paint (King, Queen or Jack) with another suited card, you can get a cheap look at the flop.

When one of the blinds, you're not in the worst position before the flop, since your blind is live and you can raise or reraise. However, in later Streets, you're always going to be the first one to act and bet, and this is a big millstone to drag around your neck.

If you have a premium or strong hand, and there have been only a couple of calls and no raises before the Flop, you want to get your raise right in then. If there have been a number of calls, let's say five calls but no raises and you hold a premium hand such as Ace - King of diamonds, you might want to slowplay for deceptive purposes when you see the flop. Suppose you see this flop:

Your Aces are very strong here. You can check, and wait to check raise when anyone bets. Of course, everyone may check behind you, but with five callers before the flop, someone is bound to bet.

What if the flop came up:

You might still check raise. No one has improved with this kind of flop and you should still have best hand going into Fourth and Fifth Streets.

If you're a blind, and you hold the same Ace King, but unsuited and the only action is from late position, with two calls, then you can go ahead and raise here. The late calls without raises increase the chances that these players have mediocre hands at best.

If you're the small blind, and still have to put up half a bet to stay in action, you don't want to play weak hands just because it's cheap, but you should think of staying in with the Mediocre Hands if there's been no raise. With a raise, you must have Somewhat Strong hands or better to put in that extra bet and a half. Check our list and try to memorize it.

## More Thoughts About Pocket Cards

Unlike 7-Stud, where, if you're dealt three of a kind in the first three cards, you have a solid chance of winning the entire pot without any improvement, in Hold 'em, no matter what cards you get in the pocket, you generally will have to improve them on the board.

There'll be times when a pair will hold up if it's high enough, or even an Ace - King, but most of the time the board will dictate the winning hand.

Aces are your best pair, because they're overcards to every other card. If any second pair shows on board then you're the winner, if no ones has trips, or a flush or straight. Aces also can win if no pair shows on board, and there's no chance for a player to have a straight or flush. That's why they're so powerful and worth raising with.

However, if other possibilities are on the board, the Aces may fade into insignificance rather quickly. Suppose the flop is this and you're holding the black Aces.

Fourth Street turns into:

The chance of the flush and straight is very great here, and if a couple of players are in there raising and reraising, you've got to figure that your Aces are now no more than a trash hand.

Another worry with the Aces is that the pair on board may give another player trips. This is more likely if the pair is higher than lower. If there had been two raises prior to the flop, it might have been enough to get out any weak pair holding, such as 6s and below. Suppose you're still holding the pair of black Aces and the flop comes up:

Let's say there are two other players in the pot and it's checked to you by one of the players. You bet and get two calls.

On Fourth Street you now see:

Again it's checked to you. You bet and then are hit with a raise, with the third player calling. It's doubtful that you're raised with an open ended straight here. Probably one player has a pair of 10s or Jacks in the hole and is now coming out betting.

From the way you've been raising and betting, you can't expect a good player to raise you with just Jacks over another pair, or 10s over. The board doesn't suggest anything else, with the exception of trip 4s or 5s. But even if this is the case, you're still a big underdog going into Fifth Street.

Kings, though very strong in the pocket, can be beaten by Aces, and that's the most logical card for any player to hold to see the flop. So, with Kings, if you see an Ace on the board, you may have only the second best pair.

Ace - King suited is very strong, for not only will it guarantee a win if the suit you hold makes a flush on board, but pairing either the Ace or King on board may win by itself. Suppose you hold Ace hearts, King hearts, and the flop comes out:

You're in a terrific position here. If a second pair comes up you'll probably win the hand. If no other pair or no possibility for another flush comes up, your Aces might win anyway. If a heart comes up you've got the nuts if no pair also shows.

However, the Ace - King suited can fade in value if there's a possible flush showing on board other than the suit you're holding.

If a straight draw shows on board, the same situation prevails. An open pair isn't that beneficial to the Ace - King suited because this holding can easily lose to two pair with a board like this, and you're holding the Ace - King of hearts.

If you have competition to Fifth Street with raises by an opponent, he may hold the Queen here and his two pair easily beat your holdings.

With pairs in your pocket, the bigger the better. The reason is simple. If there's no improvement, your pair may be stronger than any pair on the board, or drawn to by another player. If you hold Queens, for example, and the board shows:

There's a strong possibility that you have the winner here. You'll have Queen up. If someone is holding Ace - Jack, for instance, you're an easy winner.

As the pairs go down in rank, they go down in value. Suppose you hold a pair of 7s and you see this board:

Any player holding a 10, Queen or King is going to beat you. You don't have an overpair; you simply have the second pair.

2s thus will be quite weak, since you'd need a third deuce to have a chance at winning. With weaker pairs, it might pay to see the flop, but if there's no improvement there, throw them away if you have to take two or three bets to see Fourth Street. Suppose you have 3s and the flop is:

The player to your right bets and there are three players still to your left. Dump your hand as fast as possible.

Connected cards, especially if they're suited, are interesting plays. Suited, they're much stronger than unsuited and can be played much more often. For example, suppose you hold 9 clubs - 8 diamonds. Against any kind of raising action before the flop, you should throw these away. But if you hold 9 clubs - 8 clubs, you might stay in. With the right board you can be a winner, and no one will put you on this holding.

That's the great thing about suited connected cards. They add a great deal of deception to your play.

Suppose the flop comes up:

You have an open ended straight now. If Fourth Street shows:

You not only have a formed straight but a four flush working. What you'd want is an odd card of any suit on Fifth Street to gain the nuts, but a club probably won't hurt you either, with the dim prospect of someone else holding two clubs, one of them higher than yours.

If you've raised on the flop and then on Fourth Street and have only two other players in the pot, you're probably facing a two pair hand at best on the River.

The connected cards are best in the middle of a straight or at it's high end. If you hold the ignorant end of the straight, which is the low end, your hand may fall to a higher straight. That's why the weaker the connected cards, the weaker the possibilities.

For example, you hold 4 and 3 of diamonds. The flop comes up:

You have an open-ended straight, but there's the possibility of a higher straight forming, and also the two hearts must give you pause here, for any player holding two hearts is going to stay in for the remaining Streets.

Fourth Street shows:

You now have your straight. If you raise and are reraised, you won't throw your cards away but must take into consideration the possibility of a higher straight beating you.

Suppose the final board is:

Now one player drops out, probably because he couldn't make the heart flush, but the other player is in there betting. Since the 3 of clubs seems like a dead card, that specter of the higher straight still is there.

If you held the other end, the higher end, then you'd have the nuts. If someone else may be holding the nuts, then you have to exercise caution.

A word about this concept of nuts. Because Hold 'em attracts loose players who love to bluff and overplay their hands because of the complex nature of the game, you can't really play this game if you imagine that you're up against the nuts all the time. You have to disregard that concept and play your cards, but at the same time you have to be realistic about what's out there on the board.

Your opponent in the last hand saw the three to a straight and saw you raising on Fourth Street. He's putting you on a straight, and he's not coming out betting if he has inferior cards. He may, of course, do this, but it's probable that you're beaten. A **crying call** (a weak call made reluctantly) here is better than a raise.

An Ace with any other card in the same suit is a worthwhile hand because if the board makes you a flush you've generally got the nuts. So, if you're in there even with Ace - 2 of spades and the board ends up:

You've got the nuts here.

It's different with King - deuce, which is a much weaker hand in the same suit. If another player is holding the Ace and a suited card, he has you beat. In this situation, you want to see the Ace of that suit flop immediately, then your King becomes tops if a flush develops.

The side card often plays a key role in determining the winner of the pot. That's why it doesn't pay to always stay in with an Ace, no matter what sidecard you have. Even if an Ace shows on board, it may be likely that another player is also holding an Ace with a higher sidecard.

For example, you stay in with Ace clubs - 6 diamonds and the final board shows:

You turn over your Aces up and have to use the 9 of hearts to form your best hand, but another player turns over Ace - Queen and easily wins the pot.

Holding on to an Ace no matter what the sidecard, whether low or unsuited, it a good way to dribble away your cash at the Hold 'em table.

Anytime you hold an Ace with a 9 unsuited, you should throw the hand away. Ace - 10 unsuited is different, for there's the outside chance of a straight here. But many players who are losers fall in love with the Ace. They see another Ace on board with a second pair and find to their dismay that they've come in second after leading the action and absorbing reraises.

Just because you have an Ace or **paint** (King, Queen or Jack) doesn't mean you have a playable hand. If the sidecard is unsuited or is weak, you have at best a throwaway hand.

When playing pocket cards the best advice is to be patient, and then, even more patient. Play the hands you can win with and get rid of the others. To preserve your table image, you may play borderline hands in late position so that you're not classified as a rock, but even do this sparingly.

Just don't get the reputation of only playing the very strongest hands, because you'll get no action when you're in. If you win with garbage, show your cards at crucial times even if no one calls you at the River. Let the others feel you're really a loose player.

## The Flop

By having three cards dealt face upward on the flop, it makes it easier for players to consider their options of folding, calling, or raising. Imagine how difficult the game would be if the flop came at the end, with all kinds of surprises.

The flop will tell you a lot. You might have gone in with very strong cards that now have little value. For example, suppose you started with King - Queen of diamonds. The flop is:

You've got to respect the fact that someone has an Ace. You really have no hand worth playing in this situation. It would be different if the flop was:

Now you have a chance to win if you make your diamond flush. You have to stay in with your cards.

Often, you have to take into consideration the overcard you hold. The Ace is the best. Thus, if you're holding Ace - 8 of diamonds and the flop comes up:

You've paired your 8 and have the overcard that can win for you. If another Ace comes up, you're the likely winner. With a weaker overcard, your two pair may eventually fall to a higher two pair. If you hold Queen and 9 spades and the flop comes up:

You have to be careful here. Any player holding an Ace or

King is much stronger than you and a big favorite. You need either a 9 or Queen to show on Fourth or Fifth Street to have any chance of winning.

If there's a lot of action on the flop, it might be best to get rid of those cards. It would be a different matter, of course, if the flop was:

Now you hold the top pair, and are in control.

If you have a weak high card with a weak sidecard, such as Jack - 5 you can run into a lot of problems even if you flop the Jack. Suppose the flop is:

Players may be in there with a Jack - 10 or Queen - Jack, very likely cards to hold. Therefore, your Jacks stand little chance of holding up. Your sidecard will kill you in this situation. And should a Queen, King or Ace come up on Fourth or Fifth Street, you may be completely buried now.

When you're playing in a bigger game, you're up against better players, who will hold stronger cards when they see the flop. For instance, we know the concept of connected suited cards and how they can be played. Thus, when looking at the flop, we should take this into consideration. For example, players will hold connected 10-9, 9-8, 8-7s and so forth, rather than 10-8, 9-7, 8-6 etc. The latter three are really almost worthless.

When a flop comes up:

There's a possibility here that an opponent has made two pair, tens and 9s. It's more likely than if the flop came up:

In this situation it is rare for a player to be in the game with a 10-8, so respect this aspect of the board, especially the flop, and of course, the later streets. Just when you feel that an opponent's hand has been hurt by Fifth Street, he may be making his full house. For example, with a board like this:

You hold Ace - 4 of clubs. You were worried about the two straight out there, but a holding of 10-9 now translates into a monster full house, which beats your Aces over 4s easily.

On the flop, everyone still in the game gets to see three fresh cards, which may help even the most helpless hand going in. I've been in a game where a player stayed in with a 3 and 2 unsuited. There was no raise and he saw a flop come up like this:

He went on to win easily. That's why it's so important to narrow your field by raising if you have a decent hand before the flop.

Hold 'em, like other poker games, is kind to the aggressive player and will help the raising player. Sometimes, a raise before the flop, even with borderline cards, plus a scary flop, will enable you to drive out the other players.

For example, you go in with the following pocket cards and raise in late position:

The flop comes up:

It is checked around to you, and you bet out. There's a strong likelihood they'll all fold. If there's a bet and you raise, you're representing an Ace and may have them all fold. If the rest of the streets come up without a heart and any flush draw, you might not get a call on Fourth or Fifth Street.

**Flush and Straight Draws**

When you have a four-flush or an open-ended straight draw, after seeing the flop, you're not a favorite to make your hand. The odds are approximately 2-1 against you making your hand.

However, it is preferable to bet these kind of hands. You don't want to give any of your opponents a chance to get a free ride after seeing the flop and then buy a card on Fourth or Fifth Street that will beat you. You must be aggressive.

In Hold 'em, there's always the likelihood of community cards that might help someone, or give someone the nuts. You want to give the impression that you're the lucky beneficiary if everyone else is hesitant to bet. When you bet as if you've been helped or have the nuts, you put fear into the other players and force them to make decisions they'd rather not make. They'd prefer to limp along with their drawing hands, and not have to decide whether to take a single or double raise.

The appearance of possibilities in Hold 'em is more powerful than the cards themselves most of the time. What is out on the board can be scary, so if you're in a position to scare, then bet as though you have it. You'll find that the others will drop like flies and you won't be called on the River many times.

By betting strongly, you'll often get rid of players who think you've gotten the nuts even though you haven't. For example, you're holding:

The flop comes up:

Three players remain besides yourself. Two check, the third bets and you raise. The bettor and another player see your raise. Now Fourth Street shows:

It's checked to you and you come out betting. It's hard for the other players not to believe you've already formed your straight. The fact that you have the high pair on board also helps, and you may drive out a hand holding Ace hearts and 8 hearts here. He may figure you already got the nuts and will bow out, since if you have the straight, the best he can have is a set of 8s.

If you form a flush on the flop, it is still important to play aggressively, rather than allowing players to stay in the pot where they might beat you. You want to take the pot right then and there, unless of course, you hold the Ace or King of the suit.

For example, you hold as your pocket cards:

The flop comes up:

It is important to bet right out, or raise if another player has bet. You may be up against a couple of players, each holding a medium high spades, such as a Jack or Queen. It might be difficult to get out an Ace of spades or a King, but even the King holder might figure you for the Ace and fold.

In any event, you've formed the flush already, and the odds against your opponents getting the flush is still 2-1, and possibly a little worse, since you hold two spades in your hand.

**Playing Small Pairs**

Pairs of 8s or below are what I consider small pairs. They may very well be worth playing for the flop if you've gotten in cheaply or are in late position. I wouldn't play them to see a double raise before the flop, but otherwise I like small pairs. They're excellent holdings if they improve because of their deceptive value.

For instance, suppose you're holding 6s and the flop shows:

If there's been a bet and you raise, it's hard for your opponents to figure out what you're raising on. It is also a good move to check and raise in this situation. You check, an opponent bets, another player calls, and now you come back and raise. If you're reraised, I'd just call, but they're probably going to put you on every possible hand but the three 6s.

What you're probably up against is Kings, or Kings up already, and you're the favorite with your set.

Suppose Fourth Street comes up:

There's a bet, you raise and now you're reraised. I'd go ahead and put in two more bets here, by reraising.

The hand holding the Kings up probably figured you weren't helped by that 3 of clubs. If he held King - Jack, which is very likely, he figures to be a winner in his own mind. If the River is another rag, or a 3, then you're in a terrific position. Of course, he may have trip Kings or trip Jacks going into the River, but you can't count on him having the nuts. You have to analyze the hand going back to before the flop.

If there was one raise prior to the flop, or just calls, enabling you to stay in with your small pair of 6s, then there's little likelihood you're up against a stronger hand. And of course, the beauty of your cards is that it's difficult to figure them out.

What if you don't improve your holdings on the flop? Let's suppose you go in with:

The flop is :

There's too much out there against you on the flop for you to continue with the cards. You just throw them away. You'll need another 5 to stay in position to win. If any pair comes on board, whether it be Queens, 10s or 9s, then you have the weaker pair and may already be facing a full house. Or a higher pair. Or a straight.

The general rule is, if your small pair doesn't improve on the flop, get rid of them, unless you have another out, or unless you are allowed to stay in for free. As to an out, let's say you hold:

The flop is:

Now you have a bunch of ways to win this pot. A 9 or 4 gives you the straight, and it's probably the nuts, for you don't count on someone in there with a 9 and 7 against you. If you get another 7, you've got a set and that will win for you.

But, as we mentioned before, without help on the flop, the small pairs aren't going to do the trick. You'll probably be chasing stronger hands at prohibitive odds. You can't do this and be a winner in Hold 'em, or any form of poker, for that matter.

**Check Raising on the Flop**

As we know, **check raising** means checking at the outset and raising when it is your turn to bet again. Of course, if you check and everyone else checks, then you've lost the opportunity to not only raise but make any sort of bet on the flop. Worse, you're giving the opponents a free ride on the flop, allowing them to see the Fourth Street card for nothing.

Therefore, if you check with the intention of raising, you must be certain that someone will bet behind you. To know when this might occur, you must go back to the betting before the flop. If there's been at least one raise, you can be fairly certain that someone will open the betting. Let's assume the following situation.

You hold:

You were in early position and called the big blind and after two other calls, the player in seventh position raised. You called after the blinds folded and the two other callers also called the raise.

Now the flop comes up:

You've flopped two big pair and it seems reasonable that you have absolutely the best hand at this point. Now you're first to bet with both blinds out of play. You can bet, but a better play would be to check with the intention of raising.

You're in early position, and your raise then allows you to reverse the positions by getting the last bet. So you check, both callers check and the number 7 player bets. You raise.

The seven player might have a pair of Kings or Aces, or an Ace - King suited or unsuited. The others are straggling along, but one of them might be going for a flush draw with small spades. By getting in that second bet, you're giving this player a lot of trouble. He may now feel that you have higher spades, and by making a bigger bet, he's not getting as much value for his cards as he might gave with a single bet.

Let's assume that in this situation, one caller calls your raise, the other folds, and the seven player also calls. Fourth Street comes up:

You're still first. Now you can't check because you can be certain that everyone behind you will check also to look at a free River card. So here you bet.

The 4 of hearts helped no one and your hand is even stronger than before with only the River card to see. If it's a rag also and you bet you might still get one caller just to "keep you honest."

Check raising serves another purpose, and that is, it enhances your table image. It's always a pleasure to play against players who check and never raise, but simply call when it's their turn to bet. They show no deception and you can read them pretty easily. They hand around and limp in until they get their needed card, then they're out there betting. Against these players you can throw a number of hands away, if you see overpairs on board or a card that will give them a superior pair to yours.

However, by check raising yourself, you're preventing yourself from being read like an open book. Your check is now not taken as a necessary sign of weakness, but it may be interpreted as a potential source of strength. You can use it to your advantage when you have a weaker hand and want to get by to Fourth Street freely and hope to see a card that will make your hand a winner.

Therefore, check raising can be an effective tool in short handed pots particularly. Suppose you're in against two players at the flop. You hold:

You were the big blind and there was one raise before the flop, by a player in last position who might be trying to steal the pot. You went ahead and called the raise.

Now the flop comes up:

You're first to bet and check. The other caller checks and the late position player bets, and you raise. Now you're representing that the miserable flop, which probably kills everyone else, has helped you.

The late position player has to figure you flopped two pair or maybe a set of babies here. By **babies**, we mean low ranking cards. He's in there anyway, calling your raise, with the other player gone.

Now Fourth Street comes up:

You now have an interesting situation. Since the Ace is a dynamite card for you, you now check! What you're representing now is that you might have been just bluffing before to try and force everyone out, but now you're worried about the Ace.

Let's assume your opponent holds King and Queen of diamonds. He now figures if he bets on this more expensive street, he'll represent that he has the Ace and will get you out with his rather weak cards in this spot. So he bets and damned if you don't raise. If he still feels you're bluffing and reraises, you can reraise and you've made a monster pot for yourself, all because of your original check raise.

You've made it appear that you had tried a bluff, which you had, but now you're making it appear that it wasn't a bluff at all. It's double deception and you've got your opponent coming and going. It's an even better play if, as it turns out, your opponent was holding:

He figures he's got you with the bigger sidecard, even if you just bluffed and lucked out with the Ace on Fourth Street.

So, check raising must be in your repertoire. Sometimes in a short-handed game, or in a not-so-short-handed game, if the flop isn't very good for you, your check may induce everyone else to check and you get your free Fourth Street card.

The point is, the other players are unsure just exactly what your check means. After all, you're not going in with garbage to see the flop. You'll be considered a fairly strong player by your general table image, and therefore early checks might mean you're setting everyone up for a raise.

Altering your strategy, you might not raise after your check on the flop and save it for Fourth Street, where you're getting bigger bets out of the opponents. This is especially true if you've flopped a monster and are pretty sure that no matter what the others draw, you're the winner. Suppose you hold as Big Blind:

The flop comes up:

It's a multi-way game and there are some **loose players** in this game, that is, players who like to do a lot of raising and build up big pots. There were two raises before the flop, done by the loose players who you figure are **steaming**, that is, they're angry about recent losses and forcing the pot to be big. You figure your suited cards may win for you with the right flop, but you get this straight right off the bat!

You're first. What do you do? You check. Let's assume there are five other players in the pot, including the two steamers. The player to your left bets, one steamer raises and the other reraises, and now it comes back to you. Just call. Be patient.

Fourth Street comes up like this:

You check again, with three others now in the pot. A steamer bets, the other raises, and now you reraise. You might still get a reraise here. Let's assume the River shows:

You didn't want to see the second 9, because that opens the way to a possible full house, but you can take the lead now and bet out. If you get just calls, you can be sure you won the pot. If you're raised, just call the raise. As it turns out (for this is an actual hand played) you win the pot against Queens over Jacks held by one of the steamers, who goes even more **on-tilt** after this loss.

**On-tilt** means just what the words imply - the player is not standing straight and in reality, his brains are bent over. Steamers and on-tilt players are wonderful to play against. You can punish and punish them and they're still in there, bobbing up like a burnt cork in a big ocean. Waiting for more punishment.

**Bluffing on the Flop**

This can be done, but if the intention is to drive out all the other players, it is often a fruitless gesture. Often, it can be used to get them out on the later streets when the betting is double that of the flop.

There is a saying in poker - "It's easier to bluff a strong player than a weak one."

This is very true, for a strong player will respect your bets and raises, especially if he figures you to be a strong player. A weak player falls in love with his cards and is always hoping and hoping for the absolute miraculous card that will make him a winner. As long as he has an inside straight draw, or needs the last two cards to be of the same suit for his flush, he'll be in there.

Therefore, on the flop, which is still a cheap street as far as betting goes, if weak players are in there against you, you're not going to get them out unless the board is such that your raise represents a hand they know is fruitless to beat.

An example of this kind of board might be:

Everyone checks to you, and you bet. Or there have been several checks, someone bets and you raise. The board is so scary that your bet or raise represents a monster hand if you're holding the King.

Sometimes, any pair on board will induce the same situation. A board comes up:

This can be just as frightening if you're in there betting or raising. The pot might just be given to you on the flop. What might happen also is that a couple of players will limp in with you, calling your raise, hoping for something on Fourth Street that might give them a chance. They might have a lower pair or an Ace and they're hoping for two more Aces to show up. If it's another rag, and you bet, the pot might be yours without a protesting call.

Against weak players, bluffs can work in Hold 'em, because they see the board as well as you do, and what may help you hurts them, and they see no reason to stay on. And strong players may figure you're in a bluffing position and may very well see your bluff and not get out.

So sometimes there's a reversal of the maxim we mentioned. A weak player sees he's beaten and goes out, while the strong player is thinking, why is he raising here and not on a later Street if he's got that other King and two Kings have flopped?

I have noticed from watching Hold 'em being played, that in the smaller games against weaker players the bluff is more effective than in the bigger games against stronger players. That's one of the paradoxes of this complex game.

Bluffing and misrepresenting hands you hold has to be an integral part of your play because in Hold 'em, the very nature of the game calls for these kinds of play.

You must mix it up and get those bluffs in, especially in a tight game where everyone is playing close to the vest. You have to loosen them up. If you bluff them out, make sure they see that you've bluffed them. Give them the impression that your table image is one of a loose, reckless player, which, of course, it isn't. Then hold strong cards and beat them.

**Tight and Loose Players**

So, the other maxim works pretty well in Hold 'em. "Play tight in a loose game and loose in a tight game."

When you sit down at a Hold 'em table, you'll find that the game has a distinct character and personality of its own. Some games feature silent serious players who won't make a move without very strong cards. Other games are raucous affairs where a couple of players are drinking and gabbing and commenting on everything. And the play in those kinds of game is generally loose.

Or it may be a combination of both. Sometimes there are one or two players at the game who are in there raising and reraising all the time before the flop. This kind of loose game fits the strong player well, for the strong player should exercise patience and pick his spots carefully.

I've seen games in which hand after hand before the flop was **capped** that is, the mandatory three raises were made. The pots were huge and the play extremely loose.

The point is, you've got to adjust your play to these situations. Even if you feel uncomfortable with multi-raises, if you've got the cards, then you must stay in to see the flop. In that way you'll end up winning some big hands.

I remember an instance where I sat down in one of those games. The very first hand I was dealt was:

I was the small blind, and by time the bet came around to me, there were three raises and the raises were thus "capped."

The flop came up:

112

I thus had a nut flush draw. I checked, and sure enough there were three raises, with five other players still in the pot.

Fourth Street was:

I checked again, and watched the raises capped on Fourth Street. The River card was a spade, giving me the nuts. I checked, two raises came back to me, and this time I capped the raises, beating out a straight and another spade flush.

A final word about the flop. Many players will stay in to see these three cards with the hope of improving their weak or borderline hands. After all, these cards can transform the worst mess into a playable and sometimes nuts hand. If you have solid pocket cards, you can't afford to let them limp in to see the flop cheaply. It's important to raise and force them out, or at least give them second thoughts about staying in.

There's usually a lot of action before the flop, and then sometimes, no action after the flop shows. If the flop is a bad one, showing three rags, such as:

There will usually be a lot of checking, since no one was helped. It's that time that you must be creative in your play, betting and raising to force out those opponents who now are hoping that Fourth Street will help them a bit. It's difficult for players who haven't improved to stay in and see a single or double raise on the flop.

Suppose an opponent has held Jack spades and 10 spades. What hope is there for him now? Of course, if everyone checks, he'll be happy to see Fourth Street, which may be a Jack or 10, or a Spade. And the River card might help him further.

Therefore, players who merely call, and rarely raise, but simply play reactive poker, that is, waiting for the other guy to bet and raise and then go along, can't win at Hold 'em.

That's a habit you must get out of immediately if you want to be a winner. Stop calling. If you don't like your hand, get out. If you like your hand, think of raising and forcing the others out.

As we mentioned, and as anyone who has ever played the game knows, there's always some scary situation out there on the board, some flop that might give someone the nuts. The miserable flop mentioned above, with three rags of different suits, 6, deuce and 4, can flop someone a straight if he holds the 5 and 3.

Of course, one might ask, why would anyone hold those stupid cards?

A big blind might very well hold them if there's been no raises; a player feeling lucky and on a rush might hold them. That's why you can't afford to let these garbage hands in to see the flop, and must get them out by raising.

Also, don't be afraid to reraise. You can build up a monster pot for yourself that way. Get rid of the borderline and weak hands before the flop. Don't let them get a cheap peek at it.

In the long run, of course, the borderline and weak hands will be wasting money seeing the flop, no matter how cheaply they get in for a single bet. But there will be occasions when they'll hit with the flop and you don't want to be a victim of that rare moment.

The more you narrow the field against you, the more creative your plays. If you've gotten it down to head-to-head, there's only one player to worry about, and you can force him into extra bets or simply out-maneuver him.

However, if five players are seeing the flop, it's hard to do much, especially if the flop shows all kinds of possibilities.

For example, you hold:

The flop comes up:

You've flopped a pair of Kings, but with all those others in the pot, someone's bound to be there with an Ace and has flopped a higher pair, and it may be possible that someone else holds a Jack and Queen for a made straight. It's now difficult to maneuver.

Suppose, in this situation, you're in fairly late position, and someone has bet, another player has called and there's a raise to you. What do you do? You might think of folding here. You're not only chasing a pair of Aces and a possible straight, but if another spade comes on board, there's going to be a lot of betting on the expensive Fourth Street, with someone representing that spade flush.

On the other hand, if you were head up with that hand, you don't count on your opponent holding the Ace. He might hold all kinds of hand, maybe a Jack-10 suited. Or he might hold a King-Jack suited (not spades). In that situation you have the upper hand with your higher sidecard. You can represent the Ace here by raising him if he bets.

In other words, you have a chance to do something, which you don't in a multi-way pot with that kind of flop.

In the smaller games, I've seen eight players in there to see the flop, because there was no raise before it, and every garbage hand in the world had a chance to improve. In the very big games, particularly in no-limit games, most of the moves may be made before the flop, with players going all in, without seeing anything but their pocket cards.

You probably won't be playing at any one of these extremes, a no-limit or a $2-4 Gardena game, but you must adhere to the principle that no one should see the flop cheaply if you have solid cards.

The reverse is that you want to see the flop cheaply if you hold borderline cards, particularly if you're one of the blinds. But you don't want to play them if you're going to have to see a raise.

Just because you have a bet in there already doesn't mean you have to throw in another bet in a losing cause. That money is best spent in some other spot where you have powerful cards and you want to get more money in the pot and eliminate all those hangers-ons prying for a miracle flop.

Once you do see the flop, use the various strategies we've outlined in this chapter. Use deception, represent hands you might not have, use check raising to throw off the opposition. Make it impossible for the opposition to read you. On occasion, slow play and don't raise and wait for a more expensive street, especially if you're in the position of having a very strong hand that should win the pot.

### Fourth Street Play

Now you're on the more expensive streets, with your bets double the size of the previous bets. Here's the chance to get some real money out of the opponents, or conversely, to lose big money if you play incorrectly, or if you run unlucky. Therefore, you must be careful about certain hands. One of the danger signals is to see a board like this:

You hold:

You flopped the high pair on the turn, but now you have a

possible flush to worry about when that third club fell. If you're up against two opponents and both check to you, you should bet. They see the same cards that you do, and they may also be worried about you holding the nut flush.

If either hand held a made flush, they probably will bet, although a very strong player might go for a check raise here. If one of them raises and you know he's a strong player, it might pay to fold at this point. You don't really have any outs, that is, any chances to beat his flush.

A different situation might develop if you held the same cards and the board looked like this:

You now have two pair with the possibility of a full house developing. If you're check raised, it's worth seeing the raise to see the River card. If it's a Jack or Queen you'll bet out if it's checked to you again, and if it's bet, you have your raise here.

What if it's not a Jack or Queen?

If there's a bet to you, and you feel that you can win with your two pair and the opponent is trying to represent his flush but probably has something else, you can call his bet. If it's checked to you on the River, just check.

You can now see the difference between a hand with outs and one that is just there to hang up and dry. The worst thing is to get trapped between two flushes, with both feeling they can win the pot. The wisest move is to get out the minute the Fourth Street third to a flush shows and you haven't improved at all.

Position also plays a role in your strategy. If you indeed make your two pair on Fourth Street, but are the first to act, don't bet into those three clubs on board. Check.

If you've had a reputation for checking and raising, you might find your opponent checking also, even if he's made the flush, especially if his top card is fairly low. He may feel he's getting trapped. If you call his bet, on Fifth Street, he might still feel you might trap him. That's why you can't just play an ordinary game of calling bets, without using the powerful tool of check raising.

Another situation that develops is if the third card of a straight shows, especially if it's not a consecutive card but a broken one. For example, the board shows:

You hold:

You flopped two pair right off the bat, but now if an opponent holds the 9-7 or 9-Queen he has a made straight.

Suppose you're in against two players, and the first checks to you. You bet and the other folds and the checker calls your bet. Why would he not check raise you with a made straight? What would he be waiting for? He's first to act on the River. If he checks and you check he's lost a bet. And the likelihood of holding 9-7 or Queen-7 may be remote.

But what if that same player who's before you bets into you on Fourth Street? Your best play here is to raise. You can't just count on him to hold the possible straight. He may have all sorts of hands. He could even be holding King-Queen and be hoping to drive you out, and even if he doesn't, he can still make his nut straight. Or he may also hold a Jack and another pair, let's say Jacks and 8s.

If he held the nut straight, with a 9-Queen, he would be better off checking to you and then raising. But since he hasn't, you've got to figure him for another holding.

You would even play your hand if you just had a pair of Jacks.

Let's say your holding was:

And the same board showed. You hold an overcard and may be up against a pair of Jacks, or maybe Jacks up. But the straight is an unlikely distant choice for an opponent to hold.

You don't want to raise here, but check if you're first and call the bet, or call the bet if you're in last position.

However, a board like:

This is a wholly different ballgame. Now you have to play this as you would against three of a flush showing on board. There's a strong likelihood an opponent has a made straight here.

So, if you have only one pair without any outs, such as the King diamonds - Jack diamonds, you fold. Sure, there's a **gut-shot draw** (a draw to an inside straight) if you get the Queen, but that's too much of a long shot for you.

If you're holding the Jack diamonds - 10 diamonds, and flopped two pair, then you see the bettor to the River and the showdown. He may represent the straight, but could hold all kinds of other hands, such as Jacks up, or maybe 10s up. And of course, you could get lucky and make a full house, and win the whole thing.

Suppose we have this situation on Fourth Street. The bottom card pairs.

You're still holding:

The board shows:

It is unlikely that an opponent is in there against you with a 3, if he is any good. After all, what holding could he have to stay in with a 3? The most likely would be a suited Ace - 3, but the flop, although it gave him a pair, didn't help any flush draw. And if you raised on the flop, and was simply called, you can't figure him for the set of threes.

What if he bets into you now, after having called on the flop? You just call. You can still win the whole pot by getting your full house. If you raise and then are reraised, you've gotten the message and may have to throw your hand away, or get in that other bet and hope for the best on the River.

With flush and straight draws on board, you should have an out if you're up against a possible flush or draw. Otherwise fold your one pair.

If you are on the flush or straight draw, and you miss on Fourth Street, then throw your hand away unless you figure to get the nut straight or flush on the River.

For example, you hold:

The board shows:

You've missed the flush draw on Fourth Street and your Jack of diamonds won't give you the nut flush even if you hit a diamond on the River. If there are several players in with you, one other may be after the same diamond flush with a bigger card than the Jack, so you may be **drawing dead**, that is, even if you make your hand, you're still a loser.

If you held:

You've got a different situation. If the pot is big and you hit the other diamonds, you've got the nut flush and no one can beat you. Different hands, even though they have some similarities, call for different strategies.

Fourth Street play will in many ways be determined by what went on in the earlier betting, before the flop and on the flop. This is especially true, if a high pair shows on board. Suppose you hold:

The board shows:

If you had raised and no one raised you on the flop, the pair of Aces belong to everyone, with no one benefitting from them. You have the second highest possible pair, and from the timid betting before the flop, no one's represented a pair of Aces, a pair of Kings, or Ace-King, suited or unsuited.

If there was a couple of raises before the flop, then you have to suspect that someone may be in there with an Ace in his hand. This same player may have slowplayed on the flop, waiting for a second pair to show, or to get a high straight if he held Ace, King.

You've got to pay attention to the early betting, for it gives clues as to whether or not the board helps the opponents. You must stay alert to all these situations, and not let your mind drift at any time.

A tough situation develops when another Queen shows on the board when you're holding the Queen and Jack of clubs.

The board shows:

You now have a full house, Queens full, but may be up against the Ace full. It's a bad beat to lose these kind of hands, but that's the nature of Hold 'em.

### Fifth Street - The River

A lot of losers wait for that River card to somehow salvage their hands, and when it doesn't come, at Hold 'em tables all across the country you hear the refrain, "well, that's Hold 'em."

That deadly River card will sometimes hurt your chances also, but that's the nature of the game. However, you should know enough by now to not be in there always second or third best, praying for some card to make you a winner. You should have some outs, some other chances to win.

Above all, Hold 'em requires patience, and if you don't have that blessed quality, don't play the game. After all, you'll only get two cards to start with, and most of the time they'll be strictly garbage cards. You've got to throw them away and wait for the solid cards that will give you a chance to win. I can't emphasize that point enough.

Above all, don't get edgy or frustrated by a run of bad pocket cards. Wait for the ones you can play, and just fold the others.

Back to the River. Sometimes you can't help but be annoyed when that River card either renders your hand worthless, or is so scary that it makes some other player's hand perfect. That's the game.

Sometimes you're going to have to be in to the River just to see that card; certainly this will happen with drawing hands, where you're going for the flush or straight. You might have started with:

At Fourth Street you were looking at:

There's been a lot of action, and you already figure that someone has the made straight, while you're up against two pairs in someone else's hand. But if that River card is a club, any club, you've got the nut flush and are a sure winner.

But up comes another Queen and you know you're sunk by the action it precipitates.

As mentioned in our comments on Fourth Street play, be careful about your flush draws, and don't stick around to take a lot of punishment if, in the end, the flush is made by you, only to be beaten by another player with higher cards of that flush. Try to get to the River with the nut flush in hand if it hits.

The same goes for the drawing hands going for the straight. What you don't want is the ignorant end of the straight, that is, the lower end. This happens quite a bit when there's a straight draw out there, and you're in with the lower end cards.

For example, you hold:

The final board is:

You've made your straight, all right, but someone else might have made a higher straight, since a holding of Jack and Queen, suited or unsuited, is a likely hand for a player to hold to see the Flop, and once he sees it, to go all the way to the River with it.

This is not to say that you're going to be beaten with these hands all the time; what you must do is exercise caution. Don't be raising and reraising unless you have the nut straight, not the potential ignorant end. Remember, those cards on board are helping everybody, and as your hand improves, so does your opponent's.

The other way that the River card kills you is when it is so scary that you must just pray the other guy didn't hit anything. An example might be this.

You start with:

Fourth Street is:

You're up against a couple of players, one of whom is steady, and the other is on tilt, steaming over losses and staying in for every hand. What's he doing in now, absorbing your bets and not raising back? He probably holds one diamond in his hand and is praying for another on the River. You figure the other player may have a pair of Aces or Kings at this point but you've got the best second pair and aren't that worried.

All you need to collect the pot's take is to see any card but a diamond. And of course, out comes a diamond, and the steamer now goes wild. He's made his hand with this stroke of luck, and he's probably thanking the heavens for the pot. It happens.

Fifth Street play is fairly cut and dried, for most of the moves have been made on the previous streets. You might have started off with five opponents and are now down to one or two. There's still a move or two left in situations.

First of all, if you have the absolute nuts, you might want to figure out a way to get in an extra bet. That calls for checking and raising, but you must be careful that everyone doesn't check here and you lose even one bet. If you're in there against two players, the best position to be in for this move is the first position to bet. If someone checks before you and you check, there's only one player left and he might check.

You must be sure you're getting a chance to raise, and so, like all other situations, you must analyze the play of the opponents. You might have given the impression that you're on a drawing hand that's missed, and thus induce an opponent to make his bet. Or you might give him a chance to bluff you, or attempt to do so by your image at the table.

Sometimes players think they pick up tells, and if that's the case, a slight supposedly inadvertent shaking of the head when the River card comes up often induces an opponent to bet into you.

Suppose you've held:

Fourth Street shows:

Now, what you really want to see is another spade to get some action on the River. Instead, the final board looks like this:

You don't have the absolute nuts, since any hand with a pair of

2s, Kings or Aces is going to beat you, but you are fairly certain you've got the pot locked up. So the shaking of the head in disappointment that you didn't see the third spade might be real.

You check here, and the bettor might figure that you're worried about the King showing, and he throws in a bet. Or he has Aces up now and makes a legitimate bet. You raise, and may get a reraise, but most likely a simple call.

If you had bet out, after all the previous action you've given, the best that you'd get would be a call. Instead, you've got the other player figuring that you were going for the spade flush, and hold something like 10s and 2s, and you're going to call his bet anyway.

A lot of thoughts may enter his head, but let him do the thinking and make the painful decision, not you.

If you've narrowed the field to one or two players, particularly one player, and you're going head-to-head against him, and he checks to you, and you feel you're beaten, it might pay to bet if that's the only way you're going to win the pot. This is true if the last card is rather scary.

Suppose you hold:

The final board looks like this:

Your opponent checks to you. You've missed everything. You figure the Ace hasn't helped him at all. Maybe he has a pair that he made matching one of his cards with a board card.

If you check behind him, the pot will not be yours. Any pair he has, or even a King, will beat you. So you bet. If he check raises, you throw away the hand. If he calls, well, maybe some miracle

126

will allow you to win. Probably not. But he may fold!

If you're first in that situation, you can bet out and then let him make a decision whether or not to call. Since the board helps everyone in Hold 'em, there is more likelihood of players giving up the pot without a final bet on the River than there is in games like 7-Stud.

Raising is more treacherous, and I don't advise it unless you feel this is the kind of player who will fold if he feels he's beat, and isn't afraid of being bluffed out. But it's generally a bad move, since you're putting in two and possibly three expensive bets in the distant hope that you're going to bluff out someone. You're better off saving those bets for hands where you have the better or best cards.

Hold 'em is a complex game, and the more you play, the more experience you get, the better you'll play if you follow sound principles of play.

Study not only the board and the previous bets but watch your opponents for tells. If a player is eager to get his bet in, he probably has good cards. If a player must think about whether to call, keep an eye on him in future hands. You may be able to roll over him later on.

Above all, have an aggressive stance at the table. Make the others fear you. Alter your play so they never can be sure what you're up to, or what kind of hand you have. But do this within the confines of good play, not crazy play. Following this formula should make you a winner.

# VIII. DRAW POKER HIGH - JACKS OR BETTER

**Introduction**

A player must hold a pair of Jacks or a better hand to open the betting before the draw in this variation of draw poker-high.

This game can be played as a private game or as a casino game. It is rarely played in Las Vegas, but used to be one of the mainstays of the California clubs.

In the clubs, the players dealt the cards, and this is still the practice in some clubs. However, the general rule in California is to have a house dealer handle the deals. The change in popularity came about with the introduction of stud and Hold'em games, which now occupy most of the tables, with the high draw games hard to find anymore.

Whether private or as a club game, the rules are pretty much the same, except that the club game uses a joker, which has limited use. It can be used as an Ace or to form a straight or a flush. The bug, as it is called, can form five Aces, which is the absolute best hand in California high poker - draw. Thus, Aces have a disproportionate power in these games.

Let's first discuss how the private game is played.

**The Private Game**

When poker is played at home, it is usually one of several games played. The usual rule is **dealer's choice**, with each player deciding what game he will deal. The logical choice should be a game like draw poker, where position is all important, for there is a definite advantage to betting and drawing last in this game.

Eight players are usually the maximum allowed because of all the cards used up in the course of play. The deal goes around the table in a clockwise manner, with each player getting a chance to deal. We'll assume that this is the standard game played at home.

It is up to the dealer to shuffle the cards and then after they're thoroughly shuffled, to give them to the player to his right to be cut. After they're cut and restacked, he begins his deal. But before that happens, all the player must ante.

## The Ante

The ante is agree upon beforehand, and doesn't deviate during the course of the evening or day, assuming that the stakes remain constant.

A normal ante is 10% of the minimum bet. Thus, if it's a $5-$10 game, the ante would be 50¢. In a $10-$20 game, it would be $1.

The ante structure often determines the action. The bigger the ante in proportion to the bets, the more raising there'll be, for the ante is worth stealing. The smaller the ante in proportion to the bets, the less action, with players slowing down their play.

## The Betting

Bets are generally in two tiers in draw poker. The first bet, before the draw, is half of the bet after the draw, and this is usually figured by having the second bet be double the first bet. Thus games are $1-$2, $3-$6, $5-$10 and so forth.

## The Deal

After all the antes have been put in, the deal begins. The first player to receive a card is the player to the dealer's left. He or she gets a card face down and all subsequent cards are dealt face down, so that, unlike stud poker, no cards except their own can be seen by any of the participants.

After the player to the dealer's left gets a card, the player to his left gets a card and so forth, till each player at the table has one card, face down. The dealer gets his card last.

After this round of dealing, another card is dealt face down, and so forth, until each player has five cards, all of which are hidden from the other participants. Now the betting begins, if a player can open the betting.

## The Opener and First Betting Round

In order to open the betting, a player must have at least a pair of Jacks, or a stronger hand. If he has such a hand, it is not mandatory that he opens. He or she has the option of passing or checking. This is usually good strategy when the player is in an early position in the betting.

However, as each player examines his or her hand, a decision is made as to opening. If the first player has a hand weaker than a pair of Jacks, he cannot open. He must pass, or check, however, he can come into the betting later. Then the next player examines his cards and makes the same decision.

Let's assume the first five players cannot or will not open the betting, but the sixth player opens. He does this by making a bet. The bet is the lower tier of the betting structure. Let's assume a $10-$20 game. He bets $10.

Now, no other player can check and remain in the game. He has either to match the bet or raise in order to stay in action.

Let's run down a typical game, but before we do, we should note that once a bet is made, any subsequent player need not have Jacks or better to stay in the game. He can have anything, any garbage hand. Once an opener bets, then anyone can bet with anything.

- **First Player:**   checks
- **Second Player:**   checks
- **Third Player:**   checks
- **Fourth Player:**   checks

- **•Fifth Player:** checks
- **•Sixth player:** bets $10
- **•Seventh Player:** folds
- **•Dealer:** raises to $20
- **•First Player:** folds
- **•Second Player:** folds
- **•Third Player:** cold calls the $20
- **•Fourth Player:** folds
- **•Fifth Player:** folds
- **•Sixth Player:** calls the raise

Now we have three players in the game. The ante was $1, so that made the pot $8, plus the $60 bet, which made for a $68 pot. Let's see what the remaining players have:

**Sixth Player:**

**Dealer:**

**Third Player:**

## The Draw

Note that we placed the players in action in order of their bets, with the opener going first. At this point the first round of betting is over, and now there is the draw.

A player can draw as many cards as he wishes. He can discard all his cards if he desires and get five new cards. Of course, this would be extremely foolish and really stupid. But it can be done.

Now that there is a draw, the dealer first gathers all the cards folded by the players out of action and puts them to one side. Then he asks the first player to open, the Sixth Player, how many cards he wants.

Unlike the deal before the draw, all three cards are dealt at one time off the top of the deck to the opener. Now the dealer, who goes second in order, deals himself one card, after discarding the 4 of spades from his hand. Finally, the Third Player, discarding the 2 of clubs, asks for one card, hoping to fill in his straight.

Let's now see what each player has after the draw. The first player to act will be the opener, the Sixth Player.

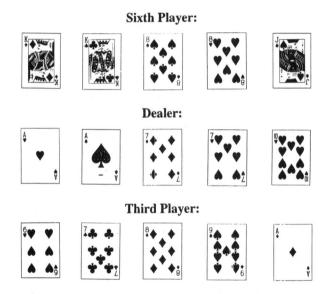

**Sixth Player:**

**Dealer:**

**Third Player:**

## Second Round of Betting

No one has improved. The Sixth Player, being the opener, goes first. He can check or bet. He checks. The Dealer bets $20, the high end of the $10-$20 game. He cannot bet less after the draw.

The Third Player folds, since he missed his straight, and the Opener calls the $20 bet.

## The Showdown and Showing Openers

The player called, the Dealer, shows his hand. The Opener, with a weaker hand, concedes, but before he does so, he must show his openers. If he didn't have openers but had the best hand, he'd still lose. This can happen if an opener made a flush by drawing one card.

Suppose the Opener shows:

He couldn't have had a pair of Jacks to open with.

But sometimes a player will discard a pair of Jacks or better and go for a straight or flush. If he does so, he must put his discard aside and not in the muck pile, to show after the showdown. This can happen when a player starts with:

He has a possible straight flush draw here as well as a flush draw, so he discards the Jack of hearts. He puts it to one side, not on the discard pile with all the other cards folded by other players. Let's assume he gets another spade and has the winning hand. Now he retrieves the Jack of hearts and shows the other players that he indeed did have correct openers.

Now that that game is over, there is a new dealer, the player to the dealer's left. He gathers up the cards, shuffles them thoroughly as all the players, including himself, put in antes, and then he gives the cards to the previous dealer to cut. The cards are then restacked by the dealer and a new game begins.

## Position

As we have previously mentioned, position is all important in the game, since certain hands can be bet in a later position that ordinarily would be checked earlier on.

We divide our position as following the first three players to bet are **early position**, then the next three, players four through six, are **middle position**, and finally, the seventh player and the dealer, **late position**.

Being in late position has a definite advantage. You can't really be bluffed there, whereas you can easily bluff other players acting before you in the betting.

For example, a player is not going to take a chance in an early position of throwing away a monster hand by checking and then finding everyone else checking behind him. Suppose a player in the Second Position holds three Aces. He'll bet.

But if everyone passes to the Dealer, and he holds a measly pair of Jacks and bets, he can make all kinds of moves against those staying in with him, knowing they didn't even have that high a hand. He can draw only two cards, giving an indication that he has three-of-a-kind, or he can even stand pat, representing that he has at least a made straight.

And he can determine just how many cards he'll draw after he sees what everyone else remaining in the game is drawing. He has, in other words, a tremendous advantage in this situation.

On the other hand, the player in early position, who got two callers, now draws two cards while the others draw three cards, and if he bets, he may not get any action on the second round if no one has improved. Or he may not get any action before the draw.

When a player in very late position opens, it can be with a pair of Jacks or somesuch weak hand, and other players might stay in, figuring they can beat him if they get a good draw.

More respect is given to a player who opens in an early position. Unless he's a weak player or a fool, he has something there that may be tough to beat.

## Opening Based on the Ante and Position

Two considerations have to be taken into account before you decide to open. The first is the ante structure, and the second, and most important, is your position.

A normal ante is 10% of the minimum bet in the game. Thus, as noted, in a $10-$20 game, the normal ante would be $1. Anything less than $1 would mean a very low ante. An ante, on the other hand, that's above $1, would be a high ante. We can consider a $2 ante as high.

When the ante is normal, or below average, then you will be more careful about playing hands and opening, especially in the early positions.

With a higher ante, you'll have to be more aggressive in opening, because that ante is worth going after. For example, in a $10-$20 game with a $2 ante, you already have $16 in the pot. If you can steal the ante that's great. But you must, even if you can't steal it, take a shot at an enhanced pot by playing a little less conservatively.

Position is the final determinant. No matter what the ante structure, you can't open with Jacks in early position. It's just too dangerous a move.

Here's why. If anyone else calls you, or raises you, then they are odds on to have a stronger hand than a pair of Jacks. You must, at that point, realize that you're second best, if lucky, and possibly third best. The reasoning is fairly simple. Let's reverse the situation, and assume that you're in Fifth position, and hold the following:

The player in the first position checked, but the number two player bet. The next player folded, and so did the player in fourth position. What should you do?

Well, it takes Jacks or better to open. Did this early position player open with Jacks? Probably not. Not only probably, but definitely not.

Even if he was a fool, and did open with Jacks, where does that leave you? You can't improve your holding by buying another Jack. You have to discard three cards and hope to get another pair, and that might still leave you second best. You just can't play the hand. You've got to realize that the opener has you beat already, and all you can do is try to catch up with a rather weak hand.

Suppose, however that you feel a pair of Jacks is sufficient to open in any position. So, you're in second position with the same hand shown above, and open after the first position checks. There are two other checks, but Sixth position raises, and the dealer **cold calls** the raise, that is, calls the bet and raise as his first bet. You decide to call.

You throw away everything but the Jacks (what else can you do)? The dealer gives you three cards. The raiser takes two cards and the dealer, one. You look at your hand:

Now you have two pair. So what? The raiser probably has a set. He drew only two cards. But you figure he's bluffing. After all, bad players play with bags over their head. So you bet. The previous raiser raises, and now the dealer reraises.

So what are you going to do now? El foldo. You don't stand a chance. You're probably up against three of kind in one hand and a made flush or straight in the other. You've already thrown in three useless bets, two before the draw and one after. That kind of play will end up bankrupting you.

In a normal ante game, in early position, you must have at least Kings to open. In the California club games, where there's a bug that can be used as an Ace, you'd need Aces.

In fact, playing at home, it might be wise to open only with at least a pair of Kings till you're in the fifth position. Then you can open with Queens in that and the sixth position. In the last two positions, you can open with a pair of Jacks.

If you're the dealer, and everyone else has checked to you, then you can probably assume that you have the best pair even with Jacks. You may not. A strong conservative player in the second seat may hold a pair of Queens. It's a chance you have to take. If he stays in and draws three cards, you're in a catch-up position.

But you're in a perfect position, betting and drawing last. You can see what he's drawing before you make a decision. If you don't improve your Jacks, you can check. If he bets, you can throw your cards away. If this particular player is a loose bettor and may not have anything, you can call. But don't be a player who's always afraid of being bluffed out. These are the kinds of players that strong poker players will send limos for to get them to the game early.

Sure, at times you may be bluffed out. Your Jacks may not be beaten, but they're not the kind of cards you want to fall in love with anyway.

When you're up against a player who's afraid of being bluffed out, you can often put him in a trap position. If you have a strong hand, a probable winning hand, and he's in front of you, and someone else has opened the betting before the draw and he called, you can raise and expect him to throw in that extra bet. The raise is correct, of course, but all evening you'll be getting extra bets at the higher level from him.

What about opening with two pairs?

Here, a lot of players run into trouble. They think that two pair is a fairly strong hand. Sure, it can be, if it's at least Queens up. That's strong to open with. Jacks up aren't that strong. You've gotten your two pair before the draw, but it's 11-1 against improving, and anyone with a higher pair before the draw who improves, has you beat.

With Jacks up, I wouldn't open in the early position at all (first three positions). I'd open with them in fourth position very carefully. In later positions, they're fairly strong and you can open with them with impunity.

In early position, you want at least those pair of ladies as your strongest pair, when you hold two pair. The higher the pair, the stronger your hand. Kings up is very very strong, and Aces up are beautiful cards to hold in any position, even the first.

What you should avoid is two-pair hands that are led by 10s or lower ranking cards. These should never be opened in early position, and you should be careful about opening them at all unless you're in at least sixth position. Again, you are facing 11-1 odds when attempting to improve them, and these kinds of hands will fall very often in Jacks or better. Anyone seeing your bet or raising you obviously has better than Jacks. After all, you opened, and someone with just Jacks is going to throw his cards away.

So, when you're up against one or two players, you are just praying that they don't improve, and there's little you can do to control the betting. You basically have a calling hand after initially checking after the draw. Those are not the kind of hands you want to play.

Let's see how this works. You hold in Second Position:

You decide to open. There are a few folds, and player number six raises. Player seven calls the raise, and the dealer folds. Now, what do you do? If you reraise and then rap pat, as though you have a monster hand, you may win by bluffing, but this is difficult strategy. You're the first to act after the draw and you don't know what your two opponents are going to do. So you just call and throw away the King and get a new card. Another King. Now you have the same hand as before.

You watch the Sixth player take two cards and the Seventh player three cards. You're first, so you check. Again, you're thinking of bluffing by betting out, but that two card draw worries you. The Sixth player bets and he's called by the Seventh player. So what do you do now? What can you do but fold? Let's say you finally make this wise decision, which should have been made before the draw, and you see the showdown between the two oth-

138

ers. The Sixth player has three 9s and the Seventh player has Aces up. You were dead in the water from the start.

In the later positions, from sixth on, the small two pair increase in value, but they're never the kind of hands you'll really feel comfortable with. I'd rather have Aces or Kings here, with chances to get a set or another pair and really have a strong hand, than to pray to overcome that 11-1 disadvantage I face each time I draw to those two small pair.

It's very important that you study this strategy in opening. Just because the game is Jacks or better doesn't mean that a pair of Jacks in your hand cries for you to open. Often, you'll be throwing them away when you're in early position and someone else has bet. In fact, in early position, if you've checked them, and anyone else opens, you get rid of them into the discard pile as fast as possible. You're up against a higher pair right off the bat, and you can't afford to play catch-up in poker and have any expectations of winning in the long run.

The more players who have checked before you, the stronger your pair of Jacks become but they can't be opened unless you're in really late position, seat 7 or the dealer's seat.

In addition to the considerations of ante you must also gauge the relative strength of your opponents and also if they're tight or loose.

Against an absolute rock, a player who needs very strong cards to even stay in, he may be passing with his pair of Kings in fourth position, and when you open as the dealer with your Queens, you may very well be second best. If you do open, and he comes back and raises you, you might as well throw away your cards.

Against a loose player, you have other options. He may be thinking of bluffing you by raising you, then drawing one card or standing pat, to carry out his ultimate bluff. You have several moves against him. You can reraise, and draw two cards, holding any kicker (odd card), and come out betting after he draws one card. He may very well throw his cards away then.

But again, you have to know the opposition, and keep alert at all times even when you're not in the betting action.

Against strong players, you have to respect the fact that when they call your opening bet, you're up against some type of fairly good hand, or a good drawing hand. Against weak players, they may be in there for the gamble, and a two-card draw by them won't mean that much. They could just as well be playing a three flush hoping for lightning to come charging out of the ventilator system and make their hand.

### Strategy After Another Player Opens

The important consideration now is not so much what your position is, but what the position of the the opener is. Also, his relative strength as a player. The stronger the player, the better are going to be his opening cards, especially from the early positions. The same is true of tight players, rocks, who will not open with anything less than Aces in the first four or five positions. Loose players and weak players, on the other hand, are apt to open with relatively weak hands even in early positions.

They may open with Jacks or Queens from the first position. They feel it's a crime to let a possible hand like this slip away, fearful that no one else will open behind them and that they've wasted a valuable opportunity. What they generally waste is their bankroll, and opportunities to lose their money.

A final consideration is just what position you're in. If an early player opens, and you bet behind him, just how many remain behind you? If you raise, are you subject to a reraise? Another thought that enters into this process is if you raise, can you drive out the other players behind you? That has to be balanced with the possibility that you'll be reraised.

If you're in late position, the seventh seat or the dealer, once more you're in a great position to make all kinds of moves you can't make in earlier positions. You know just who is in the pot, from what position they've opened and have been called or raised, and if you've been observant, just how tight, loose, strong or weak they are.

Let's give an example here. You're in seventh position and hold:

A loose player who's been steaming over recent losses opens from the third position. The fifth seat calls, and everyone else in between folds.

What should you do?

The fifth seat player is new to the game, but obviously he hasn't raised with his hand, which is probably a drawing hand. So you raise. Even if the opener has Aces, he may be loath to reraise you. Or he may reraise you just because he's steaming.

In any event, the opener asks for three cards, so he has a pair at best, the fifth seat takes one card, hoping to fill in a flush or straight, and you have a choice. You can take three or two cards.

If you take three, you figure the steamer has an inferior pair. If you take two cards, you're representing a set. If the fifth seat makes his hand, you're going to lose, but you know it's better than 4-1 that he makes it, and even better, he has to act in front of you. If the opener checks and he checks and you check, he's wasted a couple of potential bets if he's made his hand. You can be sure he's going to bet a made flush or straight.

Here's what your hand looks like after you decide to draw three cards:

You made your two pair. The opener checks, the fifth seat checks and you bet, and get a call from only the opener. He holds a pair of Queens. You win the pot. If the fifth seat player bet, you'd face a difficult choice. There may be a possibility that he went in with two pair, a weak two pair.

141

But if he didn't improve, why would he bet? You've got to figure that he went in for a straight or flush. One player has checked in front of him, the opener, who may call him with any hand, so the likelihood of being bluffed is remote.

Still, to protect your table image, you may just call here. You don't know this player and you don't want to give the impression that any bet after the draw can drive you out. Also by calling, you're forcing him to reveal his hand. If he's tried to bluff you, your table image is certainly enhanced. If he does have the straight or flush, you can mutter about never improving a lousy pair of Queens as you throw away your cards. Maybe a couple of players will take note of that statement, and later you can get to beat their brains out. Plus, there's going to be less temptation to try and bluff you out, since you've shown you don't get bluffed easily.

If the opener is a rock, and opens in early position, you've got to figure him for Aces, so any pair you hold isn't going to cut the mustard and you can throw them away. Let's say, however, that you have trip 6s as your hand. The rock opened from the number two seat and got one other call, the four seat player. You're in the seventh seat. You raise.

There's no sense in slowplaying in draw poker, since there aren't a number of streets left to make fancy moves. You've got to make your moves early. And no one sees any other player's cards. All they see are moves and judgments must be made from those moves.

You raise, the rock hesitates and then calls. The four seat player, who's weak, looks you over and throws in chips. The rock draws three cards. All right, he has the Aces. The other player draws one card. What do you do? You draw one card also. You're now representing two pair, but the rock knows if he gets another pair with the Aces, he has the top pair.

After the draw, the rock checks, the fourth seat player checks and you bet, and now the rock raises. He got his second pair. Fourth seat folds, and you reraise. Now, the rock didn't expect this. He made his two pair and you made a full house! He can't believe this. He hesitates and then folds. Ok. Or he calls. You get another bet and he concedes after seeing your trips.

Even if he bought his third Ace and thus beat you, he can't really reraise you. Maybe you went crazy and raised before the draw with a drawing hand. Maybe he figures you had a possible very high straight draw, or maybe a flush draw with an Ace and King leading it, and so you figured you had a couple of outs. In any event, you made something powerful and he can't reraise you here.

If you're in the middle position and an opener in a middle position has made his bet, you might want to drive all the other players out behind you. Let's assume you are in the sixth seat and the fourth street player has opened. Fifth seat folded. You hold two Kings with an Ace and two blanks (useless cards). You raise to drive out the two players behind you, not letting either one limp in with a low bet, since if you only call, they can call and no one can raise here. What you've done is bring the action down to head-to-head.

Whatever the opener does, you do. He takes three cards, you take three cards. He takes two cards, you take two cards, retaining the kicker Ace. If he checks and you don't improve, check. If he bets and you don't improve, now you must fold. If you improve to Aces up or to trip Kings, or possibly Kings up, you raise if he bets, and you bet if he checks.

If you merely called, and the dealer called, you've altered your position at the table from beautiful to awkward and bad, with that damn dealer behind you. If you improved and bet first after the opener checked, you might still face a raise behind you. Maybe the dealer got the trips. In any event, you're in a bad spot.

If a weak player opens in early position, or a loose player does this, with a pair of Kings you can raise him right away. Let's assume the opener is in the two seat and you're in the three seat. You raise and balance this move of possibly being reraised with the chance of getting everyone behind you out of the picture. Even if you don't drive all of them out, anyone remaining has to think -

"Geez, someone opened from the two seat, so he must have good cards, and this guy in the three seat raised, so he must really have good cards." And you'll get a crying call instead of a raise.

Now, to practice deception, if the opener takes three cards, you might take two, and come out betting if the opener checks after the draw. If neither player improved to at least a set, it might be really hard for them to call your bet. But this move may backfire against really strong players. If you're reraised before the draw by a later player, it might pay to just give up the hand. You'd need a miracle draw to win now, and if you improve to Kings up, you're probably still a goner here.

So, your basic strategy before the draw is to drive players out behind you if you're in an earlier position, and in late position, to outmaneuver the players in front of you. You've got to practice deception with your moves; remember, no one sees anything but the moves. No cards are ever seen till the showdown.

## After the Draw - Strategy

By this time, you've seen how many cards each player has taken, and what betting they've done. This should give you a good picture of what your own strategy should be after you've seen the cards you've drawn to your hand.

If you're in late position, and have drawn three cards to a pair of Kings or Aces, and the opener and another player check to you, the only way you're probably going to win the pot is to bet, if you haven't improved. If you haven't improved your Kings or Aces and the opener bets into you, you have to throw away your cards. If there's a bet by the opener and a call, or worse, a raise by another player, then you are in no position to bluff, and must discard a pair without improvement after the draw.

If you've improved your hand, so that you have two pair now, or have made a set, then a raise is in order if there's been a bet and a call. A bet by the opener followed by a raise gives you several options when it's your turn. If you have Aces up or made trips, another raise is in order here, because the raiser may be just trying to get everyone out, or he feels he might have the opener beat, or is merely representing a hand that he doesn't really have.

You've got to know the players in this situation, and sometimes, it's worth an extra bet to test them out and see how they play the game.

Other options are available to you in late position. If you've drawn one card to a possible flush and/or straight and the opener and another player check to you, a bet might drop them like dead flies from musty wallpaper. That is, whether or not you've made your hand. What you have to realize is that slowplaying doesn't really work in draw poker. There aren't enough rounds of play to set up long and involved deceptions. You've got to get your money in before the draw and after the draw.

For example, suppose there are four players remaining after the draw, and you're the third to bet. You have drawn one card and made the flush you were after. The opener and another player check to you. What can you do but bet here? If the player behind you checks, you've wasted your flush without a bet.

If you've already raised without making hands previously so that you can't really be read, by betting, you might not only get callers, but a raise. Thus a reraise gets in a possible four bets with two callers. This adds up in the long run, for extra bets in a tough game are often the difference between winning and losing.

Generally speaking, there aren't going to be that many players in the game after the draw, and most action will either be head-up or three players at the most. The very nature of Jacks or better forces this situation. Not many players are going to have that high pair or a drawing hand.

Aggressive play is very effective in this game. You already have something of a good hand to be in, and that must be respected by the opponents. Playing aggressively will force players to check to you, instead of betting. There will be times in late position when you can either steal the pot by betting, or checking and saving a bet when you're unsure that you're best. You'll be taking control of the game in this way.

Of course, tough players won't always fall for this, and will have their own moves. That's why you must separate the good from the bad players. Good players may be easier to bluff; for they'll respect your raises more than will a weak player, whose pair of Queens seem like manna from heaven to him, improved or not. Therefore, if a weak player is in with you, and has weathered a raise before the draw, and you miss your hand, you're not going to bluff him out. If he checks to you, or bets to you, fold your cards in the latter instance, and check back in the former.

Weak and loose players are ideal opponents. You're going to find some fools who will go after a flush by drawing two cards, hoping and hoping. Sometimes they'll make it. Or they'll stay in with a low pair after the opener bets hoping to make trips or something out of the hand. They have long memories, and remember saving a pair of sixes and getting a full house five years ago.

### The California Club Game
In the clubs, there'll be a **bug**, a joker, which can be used as an Ace, or to fill in a flush or straight. And that's it. Thus, a hand like this:

It's still just a pair of Kings. The joker doesn't make it a set. Therefore, in the California game, the Ace takes on added importance and value, because when you have an Ace or Aces and the joker, you have a powerful hand. It pays to keep the Ace as a kicker in a lot of hands, because of the possibility of that joker hitting.

The ace's value in the California games is the main difference between those games and the home and private games you'll be in.

There's another difference worth pointing out. In the clubs, you will be playing against a bunch of strangers if you only go there occasionally. Be careful. There may be collusion among the play-

146

ers, because in some clubs the individual participants handle the cards and deal them out. And after the draw the cards are dealt in clumps. Be alert to that fact. I'm not saying this is going to happen, but it may happen.

Before playing in the clubs, familiarize yourself with the rules of play, which are usually printed on a card you can study.

For example, if the cards are shuffled and any player feels they haven't been shuffled enough or whatever, he can demand that they be shuffled again. After the draw, the cards in the stock, from which cards will be drawn, must be capped by a chip placed on top of the stock by the dealer. And the top card must be burned before cards are dealt to players drawing additional cards. Other rules prevail, such as check and raise.

Some of these California players make a living just by finding mistakes made by inexperienced players in dealing cards and will be crying "foul hands," if any rule is inadvertently broken. Be careful and study the rules and don't break them. There's no mercy or forgiveness among the players who haunt the California clubs where there is no house dealer.

However, the day of the players dealing among themselves will probably end in the near future, except for a few of the California clubs. The giant ones, such as the Bicycle Club in Bell Gardens, or the Commerce Club in Commerce, California have no tables available for any games except dealer dealt ones.

This seems to be the trend. The dealers run the game, and they're casino employees. And high draw is almost nonexistent as a game. For example, in the Bicycle Club they have just one game, $2-$4. The Commerce Club has several, running from $2-$4 to $10-$20 and that's it.

So, if you're going to play high draw, you're going to have to play the private game for the most part. High draw can be an interesting game, and in home games, particularly if it's dealer's choice, it's a good choice because the dealer has a distinct edge in the game.

## Reading Your Opponents

Since draw poker is a game in which other players' cards are not seen by the participants, it's important that you be alert and look for the value of the opponents' hands in the way they bet and conduct themselves at the table.

First of all, try and separate the weak players from the strong ones. Weak players tend to be passive and **calling stations**, that is, they call rather than raise, especially before the draw. These players only take courage from hands that turn out well.

Betting on the come scares them. So, with this type of calling station, when he raises after the draw, you can throw your cards away if you haven't a monster hand. They are raising because they've made their own monster hand. If they didn't have a terrific hand, they'd be checking, and if you bet, they'll merely call.

There's another type of weak player who will go in with hands that shouldn't be played, praying for miracles. You'll spot them when they concede a hand to a player who lays down a pair of Jacks, after they've drawn three cards before the draw. What were they drawing to? Probably any pair, with the hope of improving.

These kind of weak players are a pleasure to play against. They'll lose their bankroll but will go home feeling good because of that one time they made a terrific hand after holding a pair of deuces.

Another form of weak player hates to be bluffed out of any pot. If this player opens the betting and you raise with a better hand, you can be sure of a call, because, God forbid, you might be bluffing him or her. Sometimes older women don't want to feel like a fool being bluffed out of a pot.

If you create the right table image, you'll get a lot of extra value bets out of this group when you have the goods.

Stronger players will have moves and will be in there with good cards. It'll be easy to spot them. Respect their play, and of course, occasionally bluff against them because they'll respect your raises.

Loose players are terrific to play against because they'll constantly be going in with inferior hands and trying to make something happen by aggressive betting. Aggressiveness is fine, when combined with good cards. With terrible cards it is a losing proposition.

And finally there are the rocks. When you're up against them, and they've opened from early or middle position, know you're up against Aces, at least. Drop any cards below that value. If they bet after the draw, they've made their hands. Fold borderline hands, like Jacks up against these kinds of players. Let the rocks have their day; often the others will know their reputation, and when the rocks open, everyone else folds as a matter of course.

Above all, be alert in this game. Study and study again your opponents' play. That's what will give you clues to what plays you should make, and if you do it right, you will be a winner.

# IX. LOBALL - DRAW POKER

## Introduction

In the California clubs this game is universally played with a joker, or bug. Thus, you're dealing with a 53 card game in which the joker can be used for any card the player wishes.

The joker becomes very powerful and it is a great advantage to have one in your hand. Besides being used as any low card, the other important feature of the joker is that it can't be paired. Pairing a small card is the bane of loball players everywhere, for it kills an otherwise good hand.

An example might be as follows. You hold the following five cards before the draw:

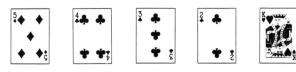

You throw away the King of hearts and pray for an Ace, which will give you a wheel, the best possible loball hand, the *living nuts*. A six or seven will also give you a very powerful hand.

But instead your final hand looks like this:

Now your low is merely a pair of crummy deuces. Your expectations of winning in a full eight-man game are nil. Someone has five odd cards against you and will beat you.

Unlike high poker, loball runs the risk, especially in five-card games such as draw, of one card destroying an otherwise fine hand. In high poker, if you go in with three Kings, the worse that can happen is that you'll end up with the set of Kings. But in loball, as our illustration showed, you can go in with a potential nut hand and end up with garbage.

Loball therefore is a game in which bluffing has some value, because it's difficult to call when you have a Jack high or have paired any card, especially if the bettor or raiser is representing a low hand of five odd cards. Like high draw, position is important, and the later the position, the better the player is situated, with the dealer having the best position of all.

In loball, flushes and straights do not make a hand a high one. They are disregarded. A hand such a 6-5-4-3-2 is a 6-5 low, despite the straight.

## How the Game is Played

In the clubs, a dealer will handle the cards. In private games, the players themselves will do the shuffling, cutting and dealing. There is a deal, then a betting round, then a draw, and another betting round. The second betting round is twice the first round. In the private games, there is generally no blind, that is, no forced bets. In the California casino game, the blind is used, and some-times as many as three blind bets are forced, before any other player has a chance to bet. Let's examine this concept for a moment.

In a $5-$10 game in a typical California club, there may be three blinds, and no antes. The player to the left of the dealer must bet $5, the player to his left must also bet $5, and the player to his left must bet $10. Thus, there is already $20 in the pot. The fourth player must call the $10 or raise another $10 if he wants to, but he is out of action if he passes or checks.

The blinds are only used before the draw.

## The Ante

In some of the California clubs, in the smaller games, such as $3-$6, there will be an ante as well as a blind. However, in the private games, the general rule is that there is an ante and no blind. Everyone antes a designated amount, usually 10% of the minimum bet. Thus, in a $5-$10 game, the ante will be 50¢.

Sometimes, at the discretion of the players in the game, the ante may be more or less. It is best to have a high ante structure, even 20%, to force the action in this game. And there's no reason why there shouldn't be a blind bet or two in the private game, since it will make it a bigger money game, with much more action.

Unlike high draw, in which a pair of Jacks is usually necessary to open, in low draw, there is no minimum hand that can open. Anyone can open the betting, so there is a possibility of everyone checking bad hands. If there are a couple of blind bets, then players will go in to steal the ante and force out the blinds.

There'll be more raising and more bluffing and more moves by the better players.

## The Deal

The deal goes around the table in a clockwise manner, with every player getting a chance to deal when it is his or her turn to do so. Being the dealer is a distinct and important advantage for it gives the player dealing the right to act and bet last before the draw. In the California clubs, where the house dealer always deals the cards, a button is passed around the table in the same clockwise fashion. The person *on the button* is the nominal dealer in terms of acting on his hand.

The dealer should shuffle the cards thoroughly, have them cut by the player to his right, and then restacked. Then each player gets one card dealt face down, beginning with the player to the dealer's left and ending with the dealer himself. After five cards are dealt face down to each player, we are ready for the first round of play. Before dealing, the dealer is responsible for seeing that each player has put in the proper ante.

In home games, a joker may be used as a wild card, but generally, the joker is not used in private games.

## First Betting Round

We'll assume that this is a $5-$10 game, with a $1 ante, played at home without the joker. There are no blinds.

The first player to act is the one to the left of the dealer. He may bet or check. If he bets, it has to be a $5 bet. Raises are also in $5 increments before the draw. If this player checks, he is not out of action. He may bet, or if the game is check-raise, even raise after another player has bet.

Check and raise adds to the excitement and skill of poker and should be used in all games. However, that rule is up to the players. But for our game we'll allow it with no restrictions.

Some casinos, particularly in Nevada, force a player who initially checked and then bet, to draw two cards. But that's a bad rule. A player should be allowed any move he can make legally in draw poker, since he doesn't see any of the opponents' cards.

Let's assume that the first four players check, the fifth bets $5, the sixth player folds, for after the initial bet a player can no longer check but must see the bet or raise to stay in action. The seventh player calls, the dealer raises, and is called only by the fifth and seventh player. All the others have folded.

## The Draw

Now the dealer picks up the remaining stock of cards and prepares to deal cards to those who wish to draw cards. The fifth player takes one card, as does the seventh player, but the dealer himself raps pat. He is not drawing any cards and represents a hand of five odd cards, headed by a low card. Now we have the second betting round.

## Second Betting Round

The fifth and seventh players check, but the dealer bets $10, which is what he must bet in this second round of betting. The fifth player calls, but the seventh player folds.

Now we have the showdown.

## The Showdown

The player who is called, the dealer, must show his cards. The other player in the game can concede without showing his, but if he has a better hand, he'll show his cards, and claim the pot.

**The Dealer has:**

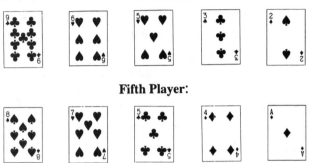

**Fifth Player:**

The Dealer holds a 9-6 low, but the fifth player has an 8-7, a better low, and wins the pot.

Now there's a new dealer as the deal moves to the player on the dealer's left. Antes are put in, and the cards are reshuffled prior to the deal.

## Opening Hands and Position

Position is of utmost importance, because a hand becomes stronger the later the position. For example, if we have a 9 **pat hand**, that is, a hand that we won't draw to, it would be foolhardy to open the betting if we're **under the gun**, that is, the player to the dealer's left and the first one to act. However, if we were the dealer and everyone passed to us, the same 9 pat hand would be worth opening and is much stronger, with a good possibility of winning the pot.

We'll divide position into three categories. There's **early position**, the first three players to bet, then there's **middle position**, the fourth, fifth and sixth players, and finally, **late position**, the sev-

154

enth player and the dealer. When opening the betting, we must be tight in the early positions, a little less tight in the middle positions, and loose in the late positions.

When we're in early position, and have a pat hand, it should be no higher than an 8. In the middle position, we can open with the 9 as our high card in a pat hand, and in late position, we can opt for a 10 high hand. However, no matter how tempting it might be, we must be careful not to find paint as our lowest card, and not to open with a Jack, Queen or King in a pat hand.

I recall watching a $300-$600 game in which a player opened with a Jack high hand in the dealer's spot and was called by another player, who eventually made a 10 high hand after trying for a 7 high hand. The opener lost a lot of money, and was called because he had a reputation at the table as a loose, and thus, weak player. By the time I stopped watching, he had pulled out wad after wad of $100 bills and lost them all.

If we don't have pat hands, we can still open the betting. In early position, we'd need a hand headed by a 7, in middle position by an 8 and in the last position by a 9. If we're the dealer and everyone passed to us, we can take a shot with a four card holding headed by the 10.

## Raising Before the Draw

As in all poker games, the aggressive player has the advantage over the passive, calling station. Since draw is a game of moves and unseen cards, and since loball enables anyone to open without having a minimum hand, there is always the possibility of representing hands that may or may not be there, and if in correct position, to outmaneuver players in early position.

And of course, there are moves to be made against loose players and tight players, weak ones and strong ones. These moves can be made before the draw to set up further moves after the draw.

If you don't raise before the draw, you're going to constantly have to get good hands in order not to be bet into or be raised after the draw. Therefore, it's important to establish a table image as an aggressive player.

Let me analyze a situation that might develop. You hold as the dealer:

Everyone checked to the fifth player, who opened. The sixth and seventh player folded and now it's your turn. You can fold, call or raise. What is best here? If you fold, you're giving away a potential winner, because you have a pretty smooth 9 draw.

By **smooth**, we mean low cards in addition to your highest card. A perfect smooth would be any card followed by 4-3-2-Ace. On the other hand, a **rough** low would be the opposite of smooth, with top card followed by something like 6-5-3-2.

Ok, so you don't fold. Do you call? It's certainly worth a call, and the probability is that the opener will draw one card also. After the draw, he'll either bet or check. You're in a good position. However, you're in a wonderful position now to influence his bet after the draw if you raise. Unless he gets himself a 7 low, he's not going to bet, and if he gets something like a 9 he'll fold if you bet after the draw. You've put him in a doubly bad position if you raise now.

If you merely call, he'll see your hand after the draw by checking and waiting for you to bet or check. However, if he misses, he's still going to call your hand because you might have missed also. You could still miss after the draw, but by raising, you're saying you went in with a real low hand and still have a very good low even if you missed your best low.

He has to make a good hand to see your bet or bet into you. Your raise accomplished one other thing, for it drove out all the other players who might have stayed for a single bet before the draw, and made your situation head-to-head with this one opponent.

Since you go last, you can also make one more move after

raising and being called. You can rap pat if the fifth player draws one card. Now he's got to check to you, and if he's missed in any way, you've got the pot, for it would be tough for him to call. If he does call and beats you, you've given the image of bluffer and next time you won't be bluffing and you'll get a few callers and make yourself a big pot.

By merely calling in late position when you have any kind of good hand allows others to enter the game cheaply. For example, if the fourth player opens, the sixth calls, you as dealer call, you may also let in one of the three early players for a cheap price. The more in against you, the more possibilities of a miracle draw beating you.

So, keep in mind those two reasons to raise before the draw. First, you're driving out other players and narrowing the field, and secondly, you're positioning yourself to outmaneuver those who are left in the game.

What if you have the nuts, or a monster hand dealt pat to you? Let's say you hold the following:

You've got 6-5, a terrific hand that should win 98% of the time. You're in seventh position and the third player has opened, and been called by the sixth player. What do you do? You raise.

First of all, there is precious little time to slowplay a hand in draw poker. But besides this, your aggressive stance calls for a raise in late position, whether or not you have a strong hand that can win it all without drawing.

By raising, the other players will still not be able to figure you out. Let's assume that only these two players call your hand. Both draw one card and you rap pat. They still remember that Queen-9 hand you stood on and tried to bluff them out with.

Now, let's say that the opener makes his 7 high hand, and the other player makes an 8 high hand. The opener bets, gets a call,

157

and you raise. You might very well get a reraise by the opener. You've made a big, big, pot with great cards.

On the other hand, suppose you merely called and slowplayed your 6-5. You still have to stand pat, and that's such a strange play that they'll figure you're trying to trap them. By being aggressive most of the time, it'll be near nigh impossible for any player, no matter how strong, to read you. And if you can't be read in draw poker, you're at a big advantage.

## After the Draw - Strategy

The very nature of loball draw is a limiting one. There are just so many low cards in the deck, and if a couple of players have them, then there's a powerful chance that the others are out of luck. In this game, there usually is a lot of head-to-head play and sometimes three-way action, but rarely will there be four players in after the draw.

So the strategy is pretty cut and dried after you've drawn your cards. You've seen how the other fellow has bet and how many cards he's drawn. Of course, if he's drawn two cards you bet or raise instinctively and punish the sucker. But you'll either face someone who's drawn one card or stood pat.

In that case, you've got to go back and remember what happened before the draw. Was he in early position, or middle position or late position? Did he open and then call your raise? Did he reraise? Were you the one that opened and did he merely call? Did he raise you?

That's not hard to remember in a game with just two betting rounds if you pay attention and stay alert. If you can't remember this, then don't play poker. Concentrate and pick up whatever information you can. This is basic stuff.

Now, you have to evaluate the player. Is he weak or strong, loose or tight?

A tight, strong player who opened under the gun and then bet right out after the draw after taking one card isn't going to lose to a 9 high hand, or even an 8 high hand. You might think he's trying to bluff and call him, but don't raise him. You'll probably be raised back and go down the drain with your 8 or 9 high hands.

A loose player can be called with the same hands, even if he opened in early position. Just because he's loose doesn't mean he doesn't have a really low hand. Even loose weak players get good hands a fair share of the time.

The problem isn't so much when you're last to act, but when you're first to act, or in the middle. Now, you have to maneuver with more finesse.

Suppose the fourth player opened, you raised as the fifth player, and were called by the dealer and the fifth player. You went in with a 6-5 four card hand, and drew a 7, so now you have 7-6, a rough 7. The opener checks, and you should bet right out. If you're raised by the dealer and then the opener folds, you should call. Reraising may get you an extra bet here, but if you're reraised, that's a tragedy, for now you're paying two extra expensive bets to see a hand that in all probability is going to beat you.

If you're the opener, and missed on your draw, either pairing up or getting paint, and you're in head-to-head with a late position player who's in a position to steal the pot by betting after you check, you can bet into him as your last chance to win the pot.

If you check, and he bets, you're a loser. If he missed and you checked and he checks also, he may be beating you with a pair of deuces while you have a pair of fours. By betting, you're giving yourself a last and final try at the pot. If you're raised after missing, don't be stubborn. Give up your cards and let him have the pot.

Your guide therefore, after the draw, is to evaluate what happened before the draw, how strong or weak the players are who remain against you, and finally, your position at the table.

We've left out your final hand, but most of the time it'll be a hand that's not the nuts or even a sure winner, an 8 high or even 9 high or 7 rough. But draw poker, when played as a low game, is one where just one card punishes and destroys a hand.

Therefore, just because you don't have a possible nut hand

doesn't mean you don't have best hand.

What you must worry about are pat hands, especially from early position, but really, from any position. Pat hands call for early raises. It's rare to slowplay them before the draw. If the pat hand is very low, such as a 7 smooth, then it should be a winner, and the bettor wants to get money in to the pot. If it's a lousy 10 high, then the bettor wants to drive the others out so it'll hold up. In either event, it's worth a raise.

A pat hand that doesn't raise before the draw is either held by a very cunning player who's somehow slowplaying, or a fool who doesn't know what to do with his cards and is overly cautious. If in doubt, don't bet into pat hands with mediocre hands. If they bet into you and you've made any kind of hand, just call.

## The California Club Game

There are two factors that set this game apart from the home, private game. First of all, there's the bug, the joker that's a wild card used as any card by the player. Then there are the blinds, which force action and make those pots really big and worth shooting at. And of course, if you're the blind, especially the big blind, you may be in the first round no matter what you hold, if no one has raised the pot.

In those games where there are three blinds, the last blind is the big one equalling the opening bet before the draw. Thus, in a $15-$30 game, the blinds will be $5-$10-$15. In some games the big blind will be double the low tiered bet, and is the equivalent of a raise right off the bat.

What this does is make draw loball into a real action game with all this money to go after. This, combined with the joker, makes for a stronger possibility of good hands with players going in with weaker hands to win those blinds right off the bat.

There's going to be a lot of action to win all that money. For example, in the $15-$30 game there's $30 in the pot (minus the rake, which would amount to $2.50) so that a player going in and calling the final blind will be getting almost $30 for his $15 bet.

160

There's good reason to have a lot of raising in these games, and for the blinds, with any kind of hand, to call a raise and try to win the pot with miracle draws.

Sometimes you have your choice of game in loball in a club. One game might be $3-$6 with one blind and a 50¢ ante. The blind is $3.

Another game might be $3-$6 without an ante but with three blinds, $3-$3-$6. If you are comfortable with a fast game, this game is for you. If you get nervous with a lot of action and prefer to slow down your play, the first game is much better for you. Of course, there will be more money won and lost in the second game. And the second game may attract poorer players, guys who are gamblers, looking for big wins by hoping for great cards.

I prefer the three blind game for that reason. The players are looser, and weak players who are real gamblers rather than solid poker players, prefer these kinds of games.

In any event, what you must do in the California clubs is respect the joker. If someone holds it, he or she is at a big advantage. It can form any card, and it cannot be turned into a pair by a bad draw. There's only one of them and you have all kinds of possible variations if you hold it.

For example, on this hand:

You hold a 6-4 smooth hand here, with the joker ending up as a 4. You've turned it into your best possible card. Now, if you held:

You get rid of the King and draw one card. If you get a 5, deuce or Ace, you have a 6 low, which should win. If you get a 7, you still have a 7-6, a really solid hand. And you only have three cards that can pair.

So it's much stronger than the same 6 low draw such as:

Here, you jettison the King, but there are four cards, the 6, 4, 3 and deuce that may pair and kill this hand. That's the beauty of the joker. Another great reason to enjoy the joker is that no one else can have it when you hold it in your hand.

With the joker and a one-card draw you should be super-aggressive in raising, and even reraise a raiser, if you can draw to a 6. If you can draw to the 5, you have a chance for a perfect hand, and the joker gives you those extra outs, with less likelihood of pairing.

Most of the games in California clubs are now run by dealers who are house employees. There are still a few of the major clubs in the Garden area that allow players to deal among themselves, but the wave of the future is the house dealer running all the games the casino offers.

At one time, loball draw was a mainstay of the casinos in California, but when the law was altered allowing stud and Hold 'em and other games to be played with house dealers running them, the loball game lost enormous popularity. In a club like the Bicycle Club, which bills itself as the biggest card club in California, about 60% of the tables are used for Hold 'em, 25% for Stud, and the rest devoted to draw games, all of which are run by house dealers.

# X. HIGH-LOW POKER - SEVEN CARD STUD

## Introduction

High-Low is just what it's name implies. Both the high winning hand and the low winning hand share the final pot, and if a player is fortunate enough to hold the best high and the best low in his hand he takes, or **scoops**, the entire pot.

He does this by using all the cards in his hand, some for high and some for low. Since the game is played mostly as a seven-card stud game, the following hand would be an illustration of holding the best cards both high and low. Here's the hand:

Five cards can be used to form the high hand, which is an Ace high flush:

Likewise, five cards, some different, can be used to form the 6-5 low:

When declaring or showing a low hand, straights and flushes do not count against it.

Thus if your hand for low was:

You'd have a 6-5 low. The fact that all your low cards are clubs, doesn't mean you have to call a flush as your low.

The flush is disregarded as a high hand for purposes of calling low. Of course, you could have called high with the same cards, with your best high an Ace high flush. Or these same five cards will stand you in good stead if you called High-Low, showing an Ace high flush for high and a 6-5 for low.

So, remember, although you can use all seven cards to form the best hands, if you can use fewer cards, that's perfectly OK also.

Another example would be the following low hand:

Although you have a straight, you can call this as a 7-6 low hand, since straights don't count against low hands. And of course, it can be called as a high hand, showing the 7 high straight.

We're going to discuss the seven-card stud game when analyzing High-Low poker. It's the most popular of the home and casino games when High-Low is played, and the use of seven cards gives the players the most leeway.

**Declare or Cards Speak**

There are two basic ways to play the game, and the first and most popular, played almost universally in private games, is the Declare game.

What this means simply is that the players declare whether they're going high or low, or high-low. It is the *declaration* that counts, not necessarily the value of the hands at the showdown, when all cards are exposed to see who wins the pot.

For example, let's assume there are three players remaining at the showdown. Two have called low and one has called high. We'll assume further that the first two players have called low and the third high. Here are the best cards they hold:

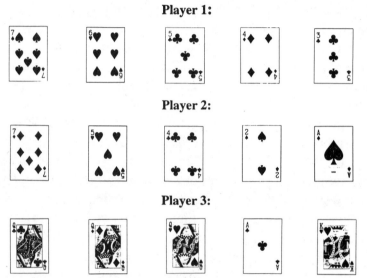

**Player 1:**

**Player 2:**

**Player 3:**

The pot is shared by Player 2, who declared low, and Player 3, the only one to declare high. Now, it's obvious that Player 1 made the wrong call, since he had a 7 high straight. In this game, Player 3 showed a set of Queens on the board and kept raising and betting with them, representing a full house that he never made. So he scared Player 1 out of calling high. If Player 1 had called high, he'd have won half the pot. But he didn't and his 7-6 falls to Player 2's 7-5 for the low end of the pot.

If this was the game played in the Nevada casinos, known as High-Low Split, where the cards speak and there is no declarations by the players, then Player 1 would have won the high share of the pot and Player 2 the low share, with Player 3 out of it, having missed his full house.

How does a player declare in this game, when declaration is the only way to go for a high or low hand? It is done after all the bets are in at Seventh Street, just prior to the showing of the cards to claim the pot. Each player at the same time should remove three chips from the table, and use one to declare low, two to declare high and all three to declare high-low.

After he has decided on his declaration, each player should put up only one hand on the table, holding the chip or chips he wishes to declare with. The other hand must remain under the table. This is to prevent controversies and possible cheating, where a player may have one chip in one hand and two in the other and hesitates just an instant before opening one or the other hand, thus gaining an illegal advantage.

The players, when declaring, should open their hands as simultaneously as possible. Then the cards are displayed.

If only one player declares high or low, he wins that share of the pot automatically, since he has no competition. If two players or more declare high or low, the best hand wins that share of the pot. If two players are tied for high or low, with identical hands, such as a 10 high straight, then they share that half of the pot.

If two or more players declare high and none declare low, or visa versa, then the best hand wins the entire pot.

If a player declares high-low by showing three chips, *he must win both the high and low hands*. If he has the best high but ties the best low, or vice-versa, he forfeits both sides of the pot and is out of contention right then and there. Likewise, if he has the best high or low, but loses the other side of the pot, he cannot share in the pot. When the high-low player is out of the pot in this way, then the second best hand wins either high or low.

If there were four people in the pot, with two declaring high, one declaring low, and the other high-low and losing high, for example, the best high hand takes half the pot, and the low declarer takes his half of the pot, even though he was badly beaten by the high-low declarer.

It doesn't matter anymore - the high-low player has forfeited the entire pot by declaring that way and being beaten for high.

If the rules we suggest for high-low are followed in private games, there will be no controversial calls. If declarations are allowed to be sloppy and not made at the same time, then there'll be all kinds of arguments and fights. Do it the way I suggest and it makes the declarations simple and sweet.

In the Nevada casino game, where the cards speak for themselves, and the best hands win automatically without declares, there is no controversy. That's probably why they don't have declarations in a casino. It would lead to fights and arguments and possible cheating by scam artists.

## The Antes

The private game should be played with an ante, for it brings more action, and involves the players in the game, where they have something to lose, namely, the ante. If there's no ante, some rock or two is going to sit on the biggest part of his anatomy and wait for monster cards. This way, you're forcing him to get involved even when he doesn't have the potential nuts.

The normal ante should be 10% of the minimum bet in a two-tier structure. Thus, in a $5-$10 game, the ante will be a normal 50¢. Anything more is a high ante, anything less a low ante. The antes are put in before the cards are dealt, and it is the responsibility of the dealer to make certain that everyone has anted, or **sweetened the pot**.

## The Deal

Each player deals, and the deal goes around the table in clockwise fashion. The deal in this game gives no edge to the dealer, for position will be determined by the cards that are displayed, with high card on Third Street and high hand on subsequent rounds being the first to act and bet.

The player should shuffle up the cards thoroughly when he or she is the dealer, then give them to the player on his or her right to cut, then restack them. Then one card at a time face down is dealt, first to the player to the dealer's left and then to each other player in that order till the dealer gets the last card on each round. A second card is dealt face down in the same manner and then a third card is dealt face up to each player in turn.

Thus, the players have two cards face down and one up. And now comes the first round of betting on Third Street, named for the three cards each player has.

### Third Street Betting

When playing High-Low, the high card usually opens the betting, whether at home or in a casino. In a casino, where there is a house dealer, and the cards are always dealt to the player to the dealer's left first, in order not to put the first players at a disadvantage, [if two players hold the same high card] suits determine the first bettor on Third Street.

For example if one player holds the King of spades and the other the King of diamonds, then the King of spades must bet first. The suits, in descending order in value are: spades, hearts, diamonds and clubs.

In the private game, where the deal goes around the table, the first King would bet, regardless of the suit value. Since the deal isn't stationary, there's no disadvantage, because everyone eventually lands in the same spot, of possibly being the first to have a high card that someone else also has.

In the casino game, a player is allowed to bet a smaller amount than the designated stakes if he's forced to open the betting. Thus, in a $10-$20 game, he can bring it in for $1, rather than $10. He can also open for $10 if he wants to, but he always has the option of bringing it in or opening the betting for the minimum $1.

Thereafter, all betting will be in the $10 range until Fifth Street, when the betting escalates to the $20 range.

In the private game, the rules may differ, but in a private $5-$10 game, the players generally must open if they're high for $5. Then all betting on Third and Fourth Streets is in the $5 increments, and $10 and increments of this amount on the later streets, beginning with Fifth Street play.

After the high card bets, then all players must match his bet or fold. Players can raise or call if they want to stay in.

Let's deal with the private game from now on, where a player has opened for $5. Other players either have to match the $5, raise by $5 or fold their cards. There's no checking or passing on this round without going out and discarding your cards.

Let's illustrate this by showing the eight hands on Third Street. The players are in order from their places to the left of the dealer.

* * means unseen cards.

**Player 1:**    * * 4 hearts
**Player 2:**    * * 10 spades
**Player 3:**    * * 9 clubs
**Player 4:**    * * Ace spades
**Player 5:**    * * 10 hearts
**Player 6:**    * * Queen clubs
**Player 7:**    * * 2 hearts
**Dealer:**    * * Queen diamonds

The Ace is held by Player 4 and he opens for $5. Player 5 folds, Player 6 calls the $5 bet, Player 7 calls, the Dealer folds, Player 1 raises to $10, and Players 2 and 3 fold. Player 4, the opener, calls the raise, as does Player 6 and Player 7.

Now we have the following players remaining; 1, 4, 6 and 7.

**Fourth Street Betting**

Now each player gets another upcard from the dealer. On this round, the player with the high hand goes first, but he may check rather than bet. However, should another player bet he must match the bet or raise or fold his cards. Check and raising is permitted.

**Player 1:**    * * 4 hearts • 6 clubs
**Player 4:**    * * Ace spades • King spades
**Player 6:**    * * Queen clubs • 3 clubs
**Player 7:**    * * 2 hearts • 2 diamonds

Player 7 is high and checks. He probably is going for a low hand and the pairing of the deuces hurt. Or he may be playing possum with trips. Player 1, who follows in the betting sequence, bets $5, Player 4 raises to $10 and Player 6 cold calls the raise as does Player 7. Player 1 now reraises to $15 for he seems to have the best low and he's making the other players pay for this fact. All the others call the reraise.

As can be seen, High-Low is an action game, because you have players going for both ends, and there are more players with shots at best hands, since they can go high or low.

## Fifth Street Betting

Another card is dealt face up by the dealer.

**Player 1**:  * * 4 hearts • 6 clubs • King diamonds
**Player 4**:  * * Ace spades • King spades • 5 spades
**Player 6**:  ** Queen clubs • 3 clubs • Jack hearts
**Player 7**:  * * 2 hearts • 2 diamonds • 7 spades

Player 7 is first to bet. The 7 of spades is a good card if he's going for low, and he bets $10. Player 1 calls since the King dampened his spirits. Player 4 raises to $20, Player 6 folds, and Player 7 reraises. Now Player 1 calls the raise, and Player 4 reraises again, capping the raises, since a good rule is to allow only three raises on any round of play to prevent collusion and trapping.

If only two players remain in the game, then the raising can be unlimited.

## Sixth Street Betting

There are only three players remaining, and each gets an up-card from the dealer.

**Player 1**:  * * 4 hearts • 6 clubs • King diamonds • 8 hearts
**Player 4**:  * * Ace spades • King spades • 5 spades • 3 hearts
**Player 7**:  * * 2 hearts • 2 diamonds • 7 spades • Ace clubs

Player 7 is still high and bets $10. Player 1 calls and Player 4 raises, to be reraised by Player 7. Meanwhile, Player 1 has to call this raise and a capping reraise by Player 4.

The pot has grown immense.

## Seventh Street or The River Betting

A final card is dealt face down to each remaining player.

**Player 1**:   * * 4 hearts • 6 clubs • King diamonds • 8 hearts *
**Player 4**:   * * Ace spades • King spades • 5 spades •3 hearts *
**Player 7**:   * * 2 hearts • 2 diamonds • 7 spades • Ace clubs *

Again the action is hot and heavy. But now, after Player 4 bets $10, Player 1 raises! Player 4 reraises and Player 7 reraises, capping the raises. His raise is seen by the other two players. The betting is over.

## Declaring

Each of the three players removes three chips from the table and gets ready to declare by placing one, two or three chips in one hand and putting this hand on the table again.

It is done simultaneously.

**Player 1**:   declares low.
**Player 4**:   declares low!
**Player 7**:   declares high!

### Player 1 has as low:

### Player 4 has as low:

Players 4 and 7 split the pot. We can easily see how deceptive the hands were in this game, for it looked likely that Players 1 and 7 would go low and Player 4 would go high.

This was heavy action and a big pot created and of course, a lot of deception. That's what makes this game so intriguing.

## Playable Hands

As with other poker games, the most important decision in High-Low is what cards to play at the outset of the game, after a player has been dealt three cards. In the private game, if he has high card on board, he has no choice but to make the first bet. However, after that decision, he must evaluate his hands.

**For his high hand, he should have the following cards:**
- Trips - three of a kind
- A premium pair - 10s or higher
- A small pair with a high sidecard, such as a Queen, King or Ace
- Three to a flush
- Three to a straight

**For his low hand he should have:**
- Three unmatched cards, headed by no more than a 9.
   The lower the big card heading the low, the better the potential hand.

However, there are other hands that are playable because of the high-low feature.
- A small pair with a small sidecard, such as a pair of deuces with a 6.
- A broken three straight consisting of small cards, such as a 7-

5-4. Notice that this hand falls into the low hand starting category.
• Any two card flush where at least two cards are 8 or below, such as Queen diamonds, 8 of diamonds and 2 of hearts. However, this is a borderline hand.

When you have the potential to take both ends of the pot by being able to call high-low and thus scoop the pot, your cards have added value. That's why it's better to have a low drawing hand rather than a high one. If you make a flush headed by a 7, then you can take both ends of the pot, but if you have a flush headed by a King, you're going high all the way.

However, even if you're going high all the way, you must consider any five unmatched cards as a potential low hand if the board shows you that this can win for low. For example, there are four players in, and it's the River. These are the hands you see:

### Player 1:

### Player 2:

### Player 3:

### You hold:

173

You haven't seen an Ace out and have a good shot at Aces full. However, the two pair on board worries you now, because he's been betting and raising since he got the second 9 on his board, and you figure him for a full house. But now you have a low to bet on: Jack-10-8-7-Ace.

The only hand you really have to worry about is the pair of Jacks, but he may have been going high all the way. Even if he went for low, he'd need three cards in the hole that were all different for him to feel comfortable with a low call. After all, your board shows 10-8-7-7 and if you have two small odd cards he knows he's doomed.

So you call low, and sure enough, the hand you were worried about calls low, but the best he can manage is a Queen low, with his final low being Queen-Jack-8-4-3. So you got half the pot, on a hand that you figured was dead for high.

Now, what do you go out with, so that you aren't trapped into betting a whole lot of money only to miss your hand? Most of the time you'll be tempted by a possible low hand.

The high hands come more rarely, for there are always a couple of blanks around in everyone's hand to make it intriguing.

For example, you might hold:

And you're dreaming of staying in and possibly salvaging a low hand here. Get rid of the cards. If the 8 and deuce were of the same suit, you'd have a borderline hand at best.

There's going to be a lot of action in this game, even on Third Street, because it's going to be difficult to get players out. They want to see another card and find out if they have a chance. If you stay with the above hand, you might get a 9 on Fourth Street. But you're still far from a winner.

Let's say you stay in and your final cards look like this:

You have a Queen-10 low, nothing but a potential loser unless everyone going for low missed and paired.

You're sure to be beaten by any board that might look like this and comes out betting on the River:

Another thing to look at when going for low on Third Street is just what cards are on board. For example, when you're going for high in regular high 7-Stud, you wouldn't stay in with a pair of 7s and a Queen as a sidecard if you saw a 7 on the board, plus an Ace and King.

The same is true when you're going for low. If you hold a 9-8-6 in your hand and you see two Aces, a 5, 4 and 3 on board, all cards you can use for low, you jettison your cards. That's five cards you can use for your low that you can't get at, because they're in someone else's hand. And one of these hands, and possibly two, may already have a drawing hand for low with an 8 or 7 as his lead high card.

On the other hand, the 9-8-6 looks great if your 6 is the low card on board, and other than one 7, everything else is paint or 10s. Now there are a ton of cards, including the beautiful Aces, to draw for.

From a hand you'd throw away, you can put in a raise here, figuring you have the lead or are now fighting only one other player for the lead to get the low part of the pot. If he draws a bad card on Fourth Street, raise till it hurts if you have an odd card smaller than the 6.

Suppose he pairs the 7 or gets a 10 or higher. He might drop here, giving you not only a clear shot at low, but a chance to keep raising two or three players all going for high, getting a monster pot out of the action.

What you want to avoid is middling hands. For example, broken straights such as 10-9-7. The middle cards will kill you in this game if you pursue them avidly. Much better to have 8-7-5 with a shot at scooping the pot if you keep getting low cards and a straight as well.

The ideal cards to hold in High-Low are not the trips, but a hand such as 3-2-Ace suited. Any three card holding below a 7 that's the same suit is ideal. You must raise with them, for you have an excellent shot at scooping the pot. With an Ace in that holding, it gets even stronger.

You can fastplay right off the bat in High-Low, because, although you may drive out marginal hands, you'll still keep in a number of players who are drawing for a good hand, high or more probably, low. The game is primarily one of drawing and you have to be alert in the later streets to see just what helps and what hurts the other players.

## Fourth and Later Streets - Strategy

If you've gone in with a borderline hand, such as 9-8-6 and miss by pairing or getting paint, you can get rid of your cards, if there's any one else out there who looks like a low draw with two small odd cards. Thus, if you're facing a 7-2, get rid of your cards. On the other hand, if you get a beauty, such as an Ace, and the 7s pair, then you want to get in a raise and possibly drive him out.

No low hand, till it's finally formed, is a sure thing. You can go in with 4-3-2-Ace unsuited and end up with a full house or nothing but two pairs. It happens, and happens a lot, so you want to get the opposition out and claim half the pot for yourself.

Your scare cards on the board should be enough for that. By **scare cards,** I mean cards that represent a very powerful hand that other players can see.

For example, if four players are in the pot, and you show the following board, how can they call low against you?

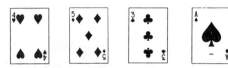

You might have a 4, 3 and Ace in the hole and have absolute garbage as a low, but how can they figure it?

That's why you've got to be aggressive. If you check this hand, or just call a high hand headed by a pair of Kings on board at the River, you might give someone else heart to call low and beat you. Therefore, since your board represents a monster low, possibly a wheel, you go and bet, and if anyone else bets, you raise.

If there's been a bet and a raise by two players fighting for high, you reraise and let the last player figure out whether to call you after he's missed his straight and only has a 10-9 as his low. The odds are he'll fold. But if you don't reraise, he might just stay in there. After all, in High-Low, just having five mismatched cards has some value in calling low.

On the other hand, if you have the 10-9 low and missed your straight, can you call a triple raise if you see that board headed by a 5. No, you can't. You've got to throw them away. It'll end up costing you four bets to hope that the one holding 5-4-3- Ace is bluffing, when any card 10 or below that he's holding in the hole will beat you.

Save your money for a triple raise when you hold the monster hand, or represent a monster hand.

On the River especially, you've got to be aggressive, especially if you're going for low and it looks like, from the betting, that the others going for low have missed or are really cautious about their hands. If all three of you left at the River are going for low, and both check to you and you bet with a board that represents low, you might have them both stay in because of the size of the pot, even if they've missed. But your bet may force them to go high, with half the pot assuredly yours.

But if you check also, even if you've missed, then one of them will probably beat you for low, and if you go for high in desperation, one of the misers might go high also, leaving you high and dry, with nothing to show for the hand.

Because of the nature of High-Low, appearances count for a lot. In regular high 7-Stud, there's the board and everyone is going one way, for high, and you can gauge the players and their possibilities much more easily. But in High-Low, the cards can come at you in both directions and you have to be alert to the betting and the play of the hands.

Does this guy have a flush for high, or are the two small cards on board really forming a low hand? In order to determine this, you must watch for signs, or **tells**, moves he makes or gestures he makes determining just what he has.

For example, I was in a game, holding a low hand, and was worried about another player.

**I held:**

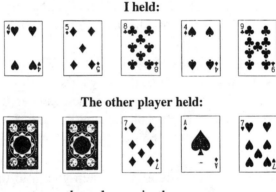

**The other player held:**

There were two other players in the game.

**One held:**

**The other:**

On Sixth Street, I was dealt:

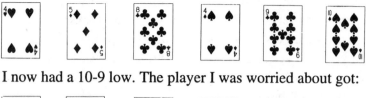

I now had a 10-9 low. The player I was worried about got:

The other two players drew:

The Jacks opened the betting, the hand headed by the King of diamonds folded, then I called, expecting to be raised by the hand I was worried about, now holding 8-7 Ace for low on board.

But he just called!

He was oblivious to the low forming on his board, and was worried about the pair of Jacks, figuring the trip Jacks would beat his trip 7s. If he had raised, I probably would have folded, because I didn't want to pay a couple of more raises on Sixth Street, then be trapped by four bets on the River, with little likelihood of winning. I could only improve to a 9 low and there was that 8 on board staring me in the face.

On Seventh Street, the Jacks bet, I raised, the 7s called, the Jacks reraised, I reraised, and now the 7s were trapped instead of me. The 7s turned out to be a set, while the Jacks had made a full house. I called low and got half of a very nice pot.

By playing passively, and more importantly, by not being alert to what was on the board, the holder of the 7s ended up paying off four full bets on the River. What this brain-dead player should have done was raise on Sixth Street when the Jacks bet. He'd then have represented a strong low hand and would have forced me out, but all he could see was his trip 7, with the chance of making a full house, and now he had to worry about those Jacks and a higher set and a higher full house.

If he had gotten me out, he'd have half a loaf instead of nothing, and if by some miracle, he got the fourth 7, he'd scoop the pot. But he had only tunnel vision and paid heavily for it.

So far we've given an overview of Fourth to River card play. Let's be more specific, and go Street to Street.

**Fourth Street Play**

If you have a borderline low hand headed by a 9 and don't improve here, but see improvement in other low hands, get out on Fourth Street. It's still a fairly cheap process and it's good play. What you don't want to do is get entranced by a couple of low cards, when you really need three low cards at the outset of play. If by Fourth Street all you have is two low cards, then you don't want to be in the game.

With high hands, you should also evaluate your situation. Suppose you went in with a middle three straight such as:

Now you buy a King of spades. Get out. You're not in a position to challenge for low, and in order to fight for high, you've got to get two perfect cards to win.

It's a different situation if you had:

And now you buy a deuce of hearts. You have a really good shot at low, and you're in there definitely.

The same holds for a three flush. If you miss out on the high side, think of dropping right away. If you miss on the low side, but now have three to a low, you can stay in. You've got a chance for a winning low hand, and if your flush comes in, you may scoop the pot.

For example, if your hand on Fourth Street is:

You're in excellent position. Any other low card on your board that doesn't pair you, and you can scare the competition for low out with a raise or reraise on Fifth Street. Now you can concentrate on getting that flush and winning both ways.

If you start high with a pair, say a pair of Jacks, and miss, you can still aim for Fifth Street play, provided you don't see a higher pair on board. But if you see Queens or higher, then it's time to leave the betting and fold. Use your common sense.

You want to win at least half the pot and to do so, you need the best cards at the showdown, unless you can maneuver the other players to give up their high hands. But not with Jacks. Aces are a different story. You pair Aces on board, and everyone may run, high and low hands.

For example, on Fourth Street you show:

It's very scary to the competition. Not only do you have a powerful high hand, but you may end up with a monster low hand. The Ace is the best of the low cards to hold.

The others might just fold because they don't want to have to guess against a final board like this:

You might have Aces up, or trip Aces or Aces full. On the other hand, you might have a 6-5 low. The reverse is true. When you see Aces on board, unless you have a very fine three low headed by no more than a 7, let the Aces have the day. And with any high hand that's weaker, you're out of play.

## Fifth Street Play

By Fifth Street, it's now possible to form a made low hand, and if you have one of 8 or lower, you're in a strong position to win the low half of the pot.

You have to play aggressively here and raise. You won't have the high hand on board, and if any high hand bets you come in with a raise. Get out the malingerers who may somehow draw and beat you even though they hold only a 7-2 at this time. Make them feel they're trapped between a higher high and your powerful low. There's just so much punishment they'll be willing to endure.

If you have four to a low now, you're still in a good position, with the caveat that you may end up missing a low hand. That's always possible. So you want to get out the competition now by raising. Otherwise the player or two going for low is taking heart when they see your board on Sixth Street look like this:

Now, if you miss on Seventh Street, any Jack or 10 low feels they have a chance at beating you, and there's no way to get them out.

At Fifth Street we have a higher betting street, so high or low, if you feel you're the leader, play aggressively and get the opposition to fold or pay extra for the privilege of seeing the Sixth Street card.

## Sixth Street Play

If you're going low and haven't yet gotten your low, don't be stubborn or foolhardy here. Unlike a high hand, which can be a four-of-a-kind hand with any pair on board, you only have two hole cards and with two little cards on board, you haven't made tiddly.

For example you hold:

The best you can have is a Queen low. Everyone knows this; it's a fact. No matter how much raising you do, the truth will not change. Now, you have to try and get into the River as cheaply as possible. You call and don't raise here.

If you raise and miss, you're costing yourself extra money. You can make extra money, of course, if you do hit, but you're not a favorite to improve. You're more of a favorite to finally pair one of your cards, and you can get a Jack as easily as you can get an Ace.

In fact, if all you see are small cards out, so that you're squeezed to get a small card yourself, you might fold if you feel you're getting rapped by a high hand and an already low hand.

Suppose you see a bunch of Aces and deuces and fours and sixes, but no 7s, 5s or 3s. Bad news coming. You're going to pair or get a card you really can't use.

By this time, you must be aware of what is out on the board, and what was already folded before and gauge your chances. If they're very slight, you don't want to give up several expensive bets just to prove the law of averages.

This goes for the earlier streets as well. If you're going for low and all you see out are cards you can use and not the cards you already have, you're headed for pair city, not lowtown.

## Seventh Street Play

Now you're on the River. Even if you missed as a low, that doesn't mean you have to get out if your board is scary enough to represent a solid low.

If you hold:

You can represent a very low low. Possibly a wheel here. After all, you have both necessary cards for that wonderful hand, the Ace and the 5. Never mind that the lousy trey paired you with one in the hole, and that your River card was another 5.

In fact, that's good. You're hiding all sorts of low cards that the others can't buy.

If you are checked to and check, you're a goner. Although you can check and raise, it's a weird way to do so with so much on your board that's frightening.

You have to bet right out. If someone else bet, you have to raise. Especially on the River, you have to get the opposition thinking and worrying. It's very hard for a 9 or 10 low to call you here.

If you've made your hand, and have a really good 6 or 7 low, bet the same way. Keep your aggressive stance either way and you'll steal a number of pots. Sometimes another low will call, or may switch to high in desperation. Sometimes you might switch also, but you want to avoid this.

You want to dictate who does what; you don't want to be just reacting.

## Deception in Betting and Declaring

The ideal situation is to have a hand that is so scary one way or another that everyone is forced to call the other way. Yet it's all an illusion - you have the other hand that they don't see.

For example, let's say your board is this:

The last 5 drove out the final guy attempting to go high. Now you're in against two players vying for low. One seems to have a 7 or 8 low and the other, if he's perfect in the hole, will have a rather smooth 7.

But your full hand is this:

You've got a powerful 6-5 low. You don't have to call high-low, just low. You get the whole pot that way. Even if the River card has missed for you, and was a Queen of diamonds, you're still assured of half the pot with a high call. You don't call high-low because you only have trips and you may get beaten high by a better hand jeopardizing the whole pot.

However, by declaring low, you have a lock on half the pot, and with this deception, probably the whole pot. The reverse is also true; a low hand that's really high. Your board shows:

You've driven out all the low competition by raising and re-raising, and by constantly getting one scare card after another. First the low players moaned, then folded. Now you're up against what looks like a possible flush and a hand that might be Queens up.

But your entire hand is:

185

You call high and you've got it all.

There are times when you'll be the victim of the same deception. That happens. But you would have lost anyway, and you lose one-half the pot. However, when you're the gay deceiver, you scoop the entire pot. Even if you didn't get the final Ace, you're going to bet as if you have the lock low, although your last card might have paired the 6s or been a King. Deception in betting is as important as deception in declaring.

Sometimes, with a monster hand that's sure to win, you might want to slowplay it at the River, as though you missed and now you're stuck, trapped.

Let's say this is your final hand:

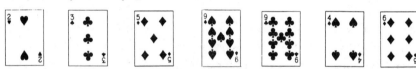

You have a 6-5 and a straight, but there are three hearts up in the air (on board) in one hand, and there are precious few hearts in anyone else's hand. You have none. But behind you are two players, one with what looks like a 7 low at best. In fact, that's the best he can have. The other has a pair of 8s showing and may have an 8 low or possibly trip 8s or better. The three hearts, with a pair of Kings on board as well, bets. You just call!

The implication is that you finally are trapped and you're praying for the 7 high hand to just call. Praying for this, so it seems. But he raises, the hearts reraise, you reraise and you've capped the raises and gotten all four bets in with your winner.

If you had raised, the 7s would have called, and the hearts might just have called. You might have a full house headed by the 9s. Otherwise why are you suddenly raising, but to trap him?

This time you don't want a player thinking, you want him to believe fervently that he has you beat for high, and the other fool to believe that you are stuck in between, but certainly not beating him. And the hand with the pair of 8s? He folded at the first sign of raising.

Your call is low, of course. You've got a lock on that and don't want to call high-low to lose everything to a possible heart flush.

The game lends itself to deception in betting and in declaring. Sometimes, if it doesn't cost you too much at the River, with everyone checking or with just one bet, you might want to go the opposite of what you think you should go.

You might have a mediocre 10 high low, but the players going for high seem to have gone into gridlock as far as confidence in their cards go. You might try a high call here, and sometimes you'll be surprised to take that half of the pot alone, with all the high hands missing and now scurrying to a low call.

But do that only when you feel you can't win if you call the way your cards look to you. And of course, you should be in at the River in this situation only if you've gotten there cheaply and absorbed no betting and raising punishment after the last card was dealt.

## The Casino Game - High-Low Split

Here we have a different situation, basically. No one declares. The cards speak for themselves. You can push people out by aggressive raising, when your board represents something, but you can't push them to call the wrong way. And you may fall to a hand that had no real chance at low but finds his King high beats your pair of deuces for low.

Thus, you have to be careful with your representations. You can represent the wrong way; that's fine, for you get all the low hands out and can now beat the high hands. Still there's going to be half the pot going to a low hand, and you may still lose half the pot to a pair of 9s.

What you want to look out for at all times in the casino game is to scoop the pot. The only way you are going to do this is to start with a low hand that goes high as well, such as a flush or straight, with five low cards around. They're your ideal hands, for the pots will get big and the wins become rather fine.

So, the strategy in High-Low split is to hold the cards that can win both ways, not to deceive as much as hold great cards. Play tighter. Play good cards and avoid borderline, mediocre hands, because you have no room to maneuver.

Remember, it doesn't matter if you deceive the players into thinking you have low and really have high. Because someone in the pot is going to take the half of the pot that goes to the best low hand and it's not going to be you.

Play tight and strong. Don't gamble in the casino game because it's going to get expensive. Play with cards that will win for you. Play to scoop. When you have that chance get as much money into the pot as possible. Make those pots big when you're taking both ends.

# XI. OTHER POKER GAMES

**Introduction**

There are a number of other poker games, which would take a volume to discuss, so we're going to limit our discussion briefly to two other stud games, one a variant of Texas Hold 'em. In addition, we'll discuss some games you may encounter at private homes, which are rather wild. The pros call them **garbage poker**, but still, you might be up against them, and should have some knowledge of how to play them.

But no matter what games we discuss in this chapter, if you've studied the previous sections and chapters, you can use the advice to good stead. Poker is poker, and a good poker player is a good poker player.

Someone like Doyle Brunson is a world champion at Hold 'em, and his best game is No-Limit Hold 'em, but I'd hate to have to play against him in Seven-Card Stud. I watched Puggy Pearson, another great Hold 'em player, cripple a loball draw game at the Bicycle Club one evening. These guys can play poker and give them any game and they'll know what to do. So should you, especially if you play most of your games at home.

You'll be involved in all sorts of games if it's "dealer's choice," and the dealer has his choice of game. When it's your deal, play a game that gives you an edge merely by position, such as draw poker or Hold'em.

Or you might play a game that the players are uncomfortable with or don't really understand fully, in terms of strategy. What-

189

ever you do, do it for your advantage. Give yourself the edge whenever you can. God knows, no one else is going to do that for you.

## Five Card Stud

This was once *the* stud game, and if you've seen enough cowboy movies, you've seen the white hats and black hats playing this game. Also, movies like it because it's simple to show, and it can be filmed so that the public can follow the game easily. There's only one down card and four upcards.

In the Cincinnati Kid, the final game played between Edward G. Robinson and Steve McQueen was Five-Card Stud. And the final hand won by Edward G. Robinson was a hand no one in his right mind would have played, but that's the movies. And Robinson won, and the kid, Steve McQueen, got his comeuppance.

This game is basically played as a high game, for there are just five cards out, and it's very difficult to form any kind of low hand. A single pair will destroy five odd cards quicker than a movie cowboy can reach for his six-shooter.

The game is rarely played today, because it's so cut and dried, and with only one hole card, there's little deception that can be practiced. If you're beat at the outset, then get out. Simple as that. If you have the best hand, stay in.

For example, suppose you were dealt:

One of the other players holds

What are you staying in for? You'll be chasing all the way. If you go for a flush or straight in this game, any single card can destroy you, and when it comes on the River, which is Fifth Street, it isn't closed as in Seven-Card Stud, but it's an open card for all the world to see. Thus, if your hand is:

Jack diamonds, 6 diamonds, 5 diamonds and 10 diamonds with the Jack as your hole card, and you buy the 8 of clubs, you've missed and you're going to lose to any Ace-high hand or any pair. You're history as far as this hand is concerned.

Sometimes, if your board is scary enough, showing four diamonds or four to a straight, you can practice deception and bluff your way to victory, no matter what you hold in the hole.

For example, suppose you hold:

You raise and reraise. The others might believe you and fold. It seems logical that you started with a Jack, possibly a Jack of hearts.

But you had to buy all those perfect board cards to get into this situation. Suppose your River card was a 5 of clubs. Then what? Any pair is going to beat your Ace-high hand.

In Five Card Stud, you want to stay in on Second Street with the best hand or the potential for the best hand. If it's concealed, all the better.

For example, you start with King clubs - Queen clubs and get:

Now your Kings are hidden and are very powerful.
Or you might hold:

And later on, get another 7 for a set. Beautiful!

This game is worthwhile against players who don't understand this principle. They'll stay in with practically anything, hoping to make a pair and win if they don't see a pair on board. But you don't want to play like that. You need patience and have to fold a whole bunch of cards before you can even get a playable hand.

Another trouble with this game is that there's little action. If one player holds an Ace, unless someone has a pair, everyone folds on Second Street. There's no money in the pot. Sometimes the game is played with an ante, and it forces a little action, but usually this game is played at home without an ante, and high card opening. After the high card opens, everyone else drops.

So, where's the fun in that? You patiently play the game for a half-hour and when you get the high card, finally, everyone else folds their cards. Frustrating, to say the least.

The only way to play this game is with a big ante, and with low card forced to open the betting. But then, you don't want to deal the game if it's dealer's choice. Why waste a big ante and a possible bring in, when your expectation is another garbage hand you don't even want to play?

### Six-Card Stud

This game is sometimes expanded to Six-Card Stud, where the first and last cards are dealt face down, giving the game more character and deception. But I'd advise sticking to Seven-Card Stud. If someone else plays Six-Card Stud high, then follow the general rules of Seven-Card Stud, with slight modifications for the one fewer card you're going to be dealt.

Since you're going to be dealt only two cards at the outset, one up and one down, you want them to be as powerful as possible. You want a high pair as your best cards, then a middle pair.

Any pair are good starting cards, but if you see them beaten on board in any early street, you fold them. You can go for drawing cards, but with only six cards you need the Third Street card to help you, or you're out of there. The odds are too great against you if you only have two to a straight or flush by Third Street.

192

You have to play a tight game to be a winner. If you get good cards, keep punishing players on drawing hands, for they're constant favorites to miss their flush or straight. Keep raising and reraising when you have the best hand and they have to draw their cards. Occasionally they'll get lucky, but most of the time you'll be collecting their money.

We're going to discuss a variation of Five-Card Stud in our section on home games. But let's now look at a variant of Texas Hold 'em.

## Omaha 8 or Better

This game is played in casinos and California clubs but rarely do you find more than a couple of tables going. Most players prefer Hold 'em to Omaha. In casinos, there is usually a single blind or two blinds. The rules for dealing and position is the same as Hold 'em. There are three big differences, however. We'll show them one by one.

In Omaha, each player gets four cards as pocket cards, not two, as in Hold 'em. These are dealt before the first betting round. The game is a modified high-low game.

For a high hand, the player can have anything, as in Hold 'em or other forms of stud poker. However, unless there's a low of *8 or lower*, there's no low.

Even though each player gets four cards to play with, he or she can and must use only *two of those cards* to form a high hand and only *two to form a low hand*.

There are five community cards on board, that can be used by all the players. They're community cards. They are dealt in the same manner as in Hold 'em. After the first betting round, three cards go out at once, called the *flop*. Then a betting round, a Fourth Street card, and another betting round.

If the game is $5-$10, for example, the bets prior to and during the flop are $5; the bets on Fourth and Fifth Street are double that, or $10. There's a Fifth Street card and then another betting round.

Then, in the clubs and casinos, there's a showdown where the

193

cards speak for themselves in determining whether a player wins low or high or takes both ends high and low. At home, there's a declare here, with players calling high or low or high-low. Then the showdown, where a player is bound by his declaration.

Let's examine some hands and boards to further understand this game.

**A player :**

**The board :**

What's the player's best hand? First of all, there's no low hand, because a player can and must use only two of his cards to form his best hand. He can't use more or less than two cards, and there's no way any two-card holding by anyone in the game, combined with the cards on board, will give a low of 8 or better.

To have a potential low, there must be three cards on board 8 or lower in value, which is not the case here.

Ok, what does our player have?

On first glance, you might blurt out, a diamond flush! His Jack with the other four diamonds makes a flush. But he must use two cards from his hand, and that doesn't give him a flush. For example, if he uses the Jack of diamonds and any other card, all can use from the board are three cards, and thus he'd only have four diamonds.

His very best hand is the two Kings and three odd cards, the 9 of diamonds from the board, plus his Jack of diamonds and a 10 of clubs. In reality he has garbage, since everyone else can use the Kings and might have a King in the hand or another pair, or might make a full house, with the following holding and the same board:

194

He uses his King and 3 combined with the board to make a full house. If he didn't have a 3 but had a blank (useless card). Instead, he wouldn't have a full house, since he can't use both deuces and the King. He can only use two cards from his hand and thus would have only trip Kings. That concept must be understood.

Often, beginning players imagine that they have all kinds of nut hands, only to find they have nothing, because they're thinking of using three cards from their hand. Understand this before you play.

Practice some dealing out of hands till you get the feel of the game.

In Omaha, we need at least three cards on board with values of 8 or lower to make a low possible. We say possible because even with these three low cards, you hand may not go low.

For example, you hold:

The board shows:

You got a terrific flop, and needed only an odd low card for your low, but missed. At best, you hold 7-3-2-Ace and you're missing another low card. You can't use the 9 because the game is 8 or better.

A 9 low doesn't count.

When going for low, the ideal holding is an Ace and a deuce, such as in the following hand:

The board shows:

Your Ace-deuce gives you the nuts! There cannot be a lower hand than this, and only another Ace-2 held by a different player will tie for low.

However, even holding the Ace-deuce doesn't guarantee anything if there aren't three odd cards on board 8 or below without a 2 or Ace. Suppose you still have the same hand as before but the board shows:

You don't have a low call here. Or if the board is:

Again you don't have a low call, because you paired both the deuce and the Ace. Your best call is high, with Aces over Jacks!

Still, an Ace deuce holding is terrific, and if two other small cards show on board on the flop, you've got to raise with them because you've got the potential nuts. If only one low card shows on the flop you try to get in cheaply to see the last two cards, hoping they're perfect for you. If either isn't, then you don't have a low and can throw away your cards unless you have a high developing.

With high hands, sometimes what appears to be a great pocket set of cards turns out to be just garbage.

For example, suppose you're dealt:

You can throw them away. First of all, you can't make a low with this hand. Secondly, you only have a pair of 9s at best since you must use two of the 9s automatically. Thirdly, you can't buy any good cards. If a pair of anything higher than 9s shows up on board, every other player has them. They can get trips or have another pair in the hole better than your 9s.

Another bad pocket is trips. This gives you only a pair, with the distant hope of getting the fourth of the same card on board, which is a real long shot, since you already have three of them. Only if they're really high trips are they possibly playable. Or trip Aces and another small card and you have an out by going low if the board lets you do it.

What you must figure in Omaha is that if there is a three-to-a-flush on board, someone's bound to have a flush, and if there's three-to-a-straight, you're going to see someone with that straight. With an open pair on board, there's the danger of someone holding a full house.

Unlike Hold 'em, where each player only has two pocket cards, now each opponent has four cards in the pocket. Out of these four, some of the players are going to have good cards.

What should you stay in with? The ideal cards are an Ace and deuce for the nut low, assuming no other Ace or 2 shows, and there are three cards 8 or lower on board. An even better hand to hold would be Aces and deuces, for that gives the possibility of Aces full if an Ace and open pair show.

Remember, just having these two pairs doesn't give you an Ace high full house if an Ace comes on board, because you can only use two cards from your hand, and the two Aces give you just a set of Aces.

Two high pair are very good, such as Kings and Queens, because you have a chance at the best full house if one of these cards show on board along with another pair.

A high pair with two high connected cards gives you a lot of play, such as:

You're happy with only two spades in your hand, because you can only use two cards, and the extra spade takes away from your chance of getting a spade flush. If you held a Jack of spades as one of your spades, it hurts your chances of getting the royal flush. For example, if the board showed:

You can't get a royal since you can only use two spades out of your hand.

Despite the four pocket cards, each player must still use two cards, and only two cards. So, if there's not a three to a flush or three to a straight on board, then no one can have these holdings. And if there isn't a pair as well, no one can have a full house. So, if you see a board such as:

There's no chance for any of those high hands we mentioned, the flush, straight or full house. Now two pair headed by Kings has a good chance to win high if no one made trips out of that board. There's always that danger. Unlike Hold 'em, any board can be a bit scary, If you hold Kings up, someone just may hold three 8s with that board. Or three 6s or three 2s. Low cards will be retained in Omaha, since there's the chance of a low.

We mentioned Ace-deuce as giving you the nut low if there's at least three to the low 8 or below on board and there's no Ace or deuce showing. Other fine low cards are 3-2 or 4-3. With these cards, if an Ace shows you have a shot at the best possible low with the 4-3, and you have the nuts with the 3-2. However, I wouldn't retain an 8-7 for a low call, and a 7-6 is very marginal.

Let's assume you do have a 7-6 and the board shows:

You don't have a low here. If the board was:

You'll end up with an 8-7 low, but anyone holding a 7-5, 7-4, 7-3, 6-5, 6-4, 6-3, 5-4 or 5-3 is going to beat you for low. Always strive to have one of the aforementioned holdings that can win for you, the lower the better. A 7 combined with another low card in your hand is very marginal. A six gives you a lot more leverage.

Once you master Hold 'em, you'll have little difficulty with this game as soon as you fully comprehend the differences. Aggression is also valuable there as in all poker games, but make sure you have a hand that's worth the raises. All kinds of hands can easily develop here, and I'd play Omaha pretty tightly, because you don't want unpleasant surprises at the River. You want to be the one shocking the other players when you show best hand.

## Private Offbeat Games

I'm being kind by calling them offbeat. Most pros consider this garbage poker and wouldn't go near some of these games. They're wilder than the games we've previously discussed in this book, with more chances to get really big hands and win big money.

There's a reason for this. The weaker players love these garbage games, because it squeezes out some of the skill from poker and allows luck to play a bigger role.

In the Maltese Falcon, Humphrey Bogart says of a punk, "The cheaper the crook, the gaudier the patter." We can say, "The weaker the player, the wilder the game."

Let's examine some of them. But before we so, we'll show the elements that make them wilder.

## The Spit Card

One card is placed out on the board as a community card that can be used by all the players as if it were in their hands. It is usually dealt with the Fourth Street Card in Seven-Card Stud, so that, if you were dealt:

And the spit card is:

You have a full house. That spit 9 of diamonds is in everyone else's hand, but in this example, it gives you the most help. The spit card is not used for a separate bet, but is dealt out before all players receive their Fourth Street card and the second round of betting is about begin.

## The Wild Card

The **spit card** is not a wild card, just an extra card that can be used by all the players. A **wild card** can be used by the players to designate any card he wishes. Usually a low card like a deuce is used as a wild card. It's popular to use this in draw poker, though stud games sometimes have wild cards. If the deuce is wild, that really means there are four wild deuces floating around. Suppose you hold, in high draw:

You now have a Royal Flush! You can use each deuce as a high club, one the Jack and the other as the Queen.

### Buying Extra Cards - Exchanging

After you've received all your designated cards in any game, usually stud poker, you can now buy extra cards, or really, exchange unwanted cards in your hand for another card dealt from the stock. What you do is dump a card and pay money into the pot and get another card.

In some games one card may be bought and exchanged this way, in other games two or three, and still other insane games allow you to keep buying cards, each for double the previous card's price, till you are satisfied with your hand. These games are usually high-low.

Let's see how this works.

Let's suppose that after you've gotten all seven cards in 7-Stud you're allowed to buy two cards. Let's assume further that the rules are, if you exchange a down card, you get a down card, and if you exchange an up card you get an up card. You are paying for this privilege. Let's say the game is $2-$4, and the first exchange card costs you $2 if it's open and $4 if it's closed, and the second costs you $4 if it's open and $8 if it's closed.

With the first three cards being your down or hole cards, you now hold the following hand:

What you're holding is Aces over Kings, and four spades headed by the Ace and King. You figure you can win if you buy an Ace, King or spade. Therefore, the only card you don't really need is the 9 hearts, which is a down card. You slide it out and pay $4. If it was open, you'd only pay $2 to exchange it. In return you get a six of diamonds. Bad news.

There's another round of betting. Now you can exchange another card. So you pay $8 and get rid of the 6 of diamonds and serendipity! You get another King and have a monster full house.

Or you could have missed, and wasted the $12 in buys. The weakies love these games, for hope springs eternal. The poor guy who paid $12 had to buy in order to win half the pot because in these crazy games, two pair doesn't cut the mustard.

There are variations of these games. Sometimes you can turn over a down card to replace an up card in buying, and get another down card. Or it doesn't matter whether you buy a down or up card - the price is the same.

Usually, in these buy games, the price doubles for each card bought in order. In one game I played in there was no limit to how many buys you could make. I had already developed a monster Aces full hand before the buys, which began at $2, with a round of betting after each buy.

I watched two hapless fools start to buy at $2, then $4, $8, $16, $32, $64. What were they thinking of? They each had invested $126 in some crummy pot and the game was high-low. I didn't invest a penny. If I had bought in that game, I wouldn't go above $8. It was senseless and futile. In the end, one of them made a best low. I took the high end of the pot, and my share of their buys was $126. This in a $2-$4 game!

Sometimes the spit is combined with the buys. That means, with two buys and a spit card, you're not playing Seven-Card Stud, you're playing 10-Card Stud.

## Roll Your Own

In roll your own, played as a stud game, the first two cards in

Five-Card Stud, or the first three in Seven-Card Stud are dealt face down. The player selects which card he'll use as his upcard. Of course, this adds to the deception.

If you are dealt:

You're going to turn the 8 up to conceal the pair of Queens. Many of these games are played as high-low, so if you're dealt:

You're going to turn up the 10, and not reveal your two low cards. It doesn't take a genius to figure out the best card to turn up.

When someone turns up an Ace, however, I get nervous, because why would he or she do that unless they had trip Aces? Or they might have a hidden pair, but still I'd rather turn up one of two Jacks than an Ace, which is very powerful, and if paired, would be best as an unseen card.

There are other ways players love to enhance the pot, but we mentioned some of the more common ones you might encounter in home games.

## Seven-Card Stud Home Games - Variations

Here are some variations that you might find. First of all, a spit card. That makes it 8-Card Stud. Then two buys. That makes it 10-Card Stud. Then you're able to roll your own. More deception. Then the game is High-Low. Now there's guaranteed action from every angle. These games can beget monster pots.

What you must be careful about in these games is the quality of your beginning cards. Just because there are all these cards, as in 10-Card Stud, as I call it, doesn't mean you should stay in with mediocre hands. Sometimes you should wait for the Fourth Street card because then the spit comes out.

Suppose you hold:

They're not very good cards, but if you can get in cheaply, you want to see the spit card and your own Fourth Street card. That gives you two cards for the price of one. Suppose the spit is:

And your hand on Fourth Street is now:

You suddenly have a powerful low hand developing from junk. However, if you wanted to see the spit and Fourth Street card and the spit was:

And your hand on Fourth Street is:

You're gone. Simple as that. Those two cards on Fourth Street can transform a lot of hands, and I usually stay in for them unless I know nothing at all will help me. After that Street, I gauge my possibilities. If I don't have a really good chance for low, or if my high is mediocre, I fold.

I've been in seven and eight-handed games and found myself the only one to fold! The others wanted to get to the River so they could buy more cards. Anything was possible, they felt.

With a 10-Card Stud, you must have a full house to be in contention at the end of it all, and you should have a pretty high full house. The low full houses, 8 or below, can just be mediocre hands in this game. A flush? On rare occasions it'll hold up. A straight? Forget about it.

The worst cards to hold in this game, if played as a high-low game, are the middle cards, the 8s through 10s. They can't help you for low, and they're not much better for high unless you get trips pretty early. Otherwise, dump them.

When the game features three buys or unlimited buys, then you want to make sure you have very powerful cards, either high or low by the time the buying comes. If you must buy, the buy should give you the nuts, otherwise drop out. You don't want to end up with a 7-5 low and be beaten by a 6-4 after you've invested a whole lot of money.

And if you have trip 6s and already see that a player is going crazy with a pair of 8s in the air, why are you in there?

Play the game patiently. Don't fall into the trap of hoping that the buys will transform your hand. By the time you're at the River, before the buy, you should have a chance to win either high or low. There should be only one essential card you need. Or you might be going to scoop the pot and although you have the best low, you want that high also.

For example, in a game with a spit, and two buys, you hold:

The spit is:

Your 6-4 low looks like the nuts against four other players, but now you have a chance to get the nut high as well if you pair any card. You get rid of the only card you can, the Queen, and buy a card. Let's say it's a 10. No help.

There's a round of betting, where you can still raise and re-raise. You've got the nut low. You buy another card. It's open and it's the 6 of diamonds! Now you have both ends of the pot. Even if you missed, it was well worth the try.

Sometimes these games are played with one spit and one buy. That's closer to regular 7 Stud, because it's only 9-Card Stud.

Or sometimes the game is High-Low, but 8 or better for low is the rule and it's played with one spit and one buy. It doesn't really matter and shouldn't to you. Go in with strong cards and realize that you need powerful hands to win. And let the others draw and buy cards, while you'll only buy for nut hands and to scoop the pot. Even then you won't buy if your chances are nil.

If you're going for that Ace and you must go for the **case Ace**, (last Ace), it might not be worth it. Or you're going for low, and all the low cards you need seem to be on the board, so that your chances are greatly diminished. Play the percentages. Don't invest in the buys if there's little chance you'll buy what you need.

## Five-Card Stud Home Games -Variations

This game is rarely played at home or in casinos, but some-times it's juiced up into an interesting game. The first two cards are dealt face down, so it's *roll your own*. Then, after all five cards have been dealt out, you can buy two additional cards. The game is high-low. This turns the game into a 7-Card Stud game of sorts, and there are good opportunities to scoop the pot here by going high and low.

For example, you end up with:

You have a great low, 6-5, and a straight as well. You can call high-low, since the straight doesn't count against a low call, and here have a great chance to scoop the pot.

What you want to do in this game is at least play for one side of the other, high or low. Thus, you wouldn't play the following hand at all:

What you're also looking for is a trap situation, where the others are going one way and you're heading the other way. This usually works when you're going for low and hold:

Let's assume you bought one card and that was the King. Now there's betting before the second buy and three others are in the game. You're in last position, the others in order of betting:

### Hand One

### Hand Two

### Hand Three

The Queen checks, the 10s check, the Jacks bet, and you raise. You've got the Queens beat for low. The 10s might be four spades at this point, and even if the 10 of clubs is dumped, you have the best low. And the Jacks might be four clubs headed by the Ace, or maybe Aces up. If he goes for the clubs, why is he betting?

He reraises you and you put in a final reraise. You're in good position to do this, for you go last in buying as well.

The Queens dump the Jack of hearts. No surprise here. The 10s dump the club 10 and goes for the spade flush. The Jacks now dump the 8 of clubs and probably has Aces up. You don't have to buy. You have a lock for low.

In this game, if you throw away your hole card, you get another hole card. But if you throw away an open card you can get it open, or you can turn up the hole card, and buy your card closed. Let's assume that the Jacks threw away the Jack of diamonds and put up his hole card and you saw:

Now you have to buy, because you may be easily beaten by the Jack hand. You get rid of the King of hearts and turn over your 8 of spades showing:

You're up against:

**Hand One**

## Hand Two

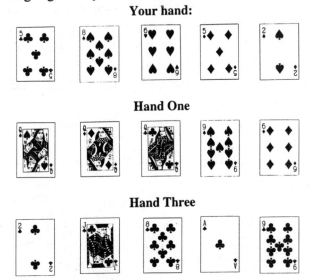

## Hand Three

The Queens check, the 10s check, the four-club flush bets, you raise and the Queens call the raise, the 10s fold and the clubs reraise. Now you reraise, and both hands call, since the raises were capped at three.

By reraising, you're forcing the clubs to go high if his club flush was made, but not high-low, assuming he bought any club below the Jack. You're representing a lock low with your betting.

The final hands, when open, with the Queens and the four clubs calling high and you calling low are:

### Your hand:

### Hand One

### Hand Three

You missed, and paired, but your betting stopped the clubs

from going high-low. He figured he had half the pot locked up with a lot of action. You could have made your low in any number of ways and killed him for low if he called high-low.

If you had merely called here, the clubs would probably have tried to scoop the pot. That's why, in these games and in all poker, if your board is scary and you bet it aggressively, good things are going to happen to you.

## Draw Poker Games - Variations

These games are more straightforward, but with the addition of a wild card, they can get really hairy. What you want to do is hold one or more of these wild cards, otherwise be cautious in your betting. The wild card concept throws regular poker awry, and you may not be comfortable with it and avoid it by throwing away your cards if you're uncertain about the play.

When you hold the wild card, and it really helps you, then go all out. If you have a monster hand without it, you can bet it. Otherwise, proceed with caution.

Sometimes, even without a wild card, a five card draw game at home is played as a high-low game, with anything opening. Play the high aspect of the game just as you would play regular high poker, and the low aspect as you would play low poker. Then you're on solid ground. What you're looking for here is to scoop the pot with a low flush or low straight. Thus an ideal hand in high-low draw would be:

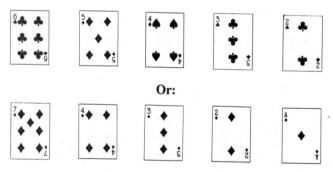

Or:

- with both an Ace-high diamond hand and a 7-smooth low.

When you're dealing, try to limit the wildness of the games, unless you feel you're up against absolute weakies and wild gamblers. Then make the games as wild as you dare, and play tightly. Let them gamble and ruin themselves; you must wait for your spots and then hammer them with aggressive betting.

# XII. A FINAL WINNING WORD

As we mentioned at the beginning of the book, the only reason to play poker seriously is to win money at it. Playing well is the way to do this. There is a satisfaction in knowing that you're playing at your best, in being recognized as a solid tough player. And the final reward is that you're going to beat the other players and take their money.

If you play at home, you're going to find the games possibly smaller but the action wilder. Adjust for that. It shouldn't be difficult to figure out the various levels of play these players bring to the game. If they're weak or loose or pure gamblers, you can make a lot of money, because they're going to give you a lot of action. If they're tight and tough, you're going to have to adjust your game to take this into consideration, but you can still make some moves against them. They're in the book, and they'll show up in the practical playing of hands.

In the home games, when you're tough and a constant winner, you won't offend anyone. They'll come back for more of the same punishment, no matter how good you are, no matter how much of a better game you play.

Most poker players think that luck is the main ingredient of the game. Their attitude is "anyone can be a winner if they get good cards." That's not really the truth, because the solid player will win much more with good cards, and will lose less with bad cards. The weak player won't get very much out of his good hands, and he'll play many more bad hands and lose much more than a fine poker player.

Everyone in the end will get the same number of good hands over the course of a poker career. And the same number of bad hands. It's what we do with those hands that separates the winners from the losers.

If you decide to play in the clubs or casinos, then the game changes. You're up against strangers, and you have to be alert to their style and level of play. You must pick it up fast by watching and studying their bets and their moves. Plus their gestures. Learn tells. We mentioned earlier how weak players do the opposite of what they think should be done. With a terrific hand they grudgingly make a bet. With a lousy hand they're throwing in the chips with abandon. That shouldn't fool you.

Listen to what they say. Some players will talk about a flush draw when they're going for two pair. Others will talk about getting that second pair when they need another spade to complete the flush. Their attempts at deception are laughable. See just what they showdown after their inane patter. See what matches and what doesn't.

A player will rarely talk about what he needs during the game, when there's still betting rounds. What he'll try and do is deceive. It should be transparent to you.

You might want to have your own patter. I used to watch the big games of 7-Stud at the Mirage in Las Vegas. A couple of great players were in these games, and when I say great, I mean great. They were superstars. And a funny thing is, their mouths never stopped working. They'd be commenting on other players hands, asking other players direct questions.

Of course, they didn't expect a direct answer when they asked if some poor tourist made his full house yet. Or is he going for a straight? But whatever the response, they picked up on a tell, letting themselves know if he indeed was going for the straight, or was the guy in the checkered coat from Dubuque really set with his full house?

Asking a direct question has its dividends. When some fool is trying to trick me by saying he gets one more heart and he's got the flush, I ask him if it matters that I hold the Ace and King of hearts in the hole. The jerk didn't expect that question. I watch his reaction. I also ask if a player has made his hand, or is he going for high or low. Some answer is usually forthcoming, and even silence is an answer.

Sometimes a player gets really flustered if you guess right. You ask "you're really looking for another 10, aren't you?" And if I hit the nail on the head, he starts to blush. Even if there's no tell, you're intimidating them, throwing them on tilt. That's worthwhile also. I'm not saying you should be obnoxious, but you can keep them off balance with questions.

What if they ask you questions? Answer them. "You made the full house, didn't you?" I'm asked. "Not yet, but I'm working on it," I answer, peeking at my hole card. "Now, be there baby," I say, squeezing the card gently. Maybe I'm going for two pair, and then why is he asking me this question? The bastard's got a flush already.

Sometimes, as is my habit, I just blurt out, "I can't believe this card," as I see my river card. Most players take that for a miss, but usually when I say it, I really am telling the truth. The third Ace came out of nowhere. And sometimes I say it when I miss. The opponents are going to figure they have a tell on me, for I said it when I made a hand last time, and they figure the same thing is happening.

I've also practiced a disgusted subtle shaking of the head combined with a tightening of the lips when I make a monster hand. Or just the tightening of the lips, very subtly. My gestures tell the other players that I missed my hand. They think they inadvertently stumbled on my tell. Why? Because I did the same thing when I missed before and had no intention of making a bet. Keep them guessing.

In home games it's easy to find tells. There's one player I used to play against who would moan and slap the river card, and then I knew automatically he was coming in for a raise. Everytime he moaned and did the slapping routine I got ready to fold. He also would sometimes nod his head and shake his fist and say, "yes!!!" That called for a raise on my part. He'd been doing the same thing for ten years and I couldn't understand why no one else picked up on it. Most of the players kept on believing his gestures were real.

In the club and casino games, try a few different games till you find the one you can play best and can make money at. Start low but not too low. If you're going to try your luck in 7-Stud, don't play the absolutely lowest games, such as $1 - $2.

Try at least a $1 - $4 in Las Vegas or $2 - $4 in California just to get your feet wet. There's a big rake of 10% which makes it hard to beat. And the players are so bad that no matter how subtly you play and no matter what moves you're making, it means nothing. You can't get them out, and they'll end up drawing out on you. So what, they think, it's only a $2 bet to see the River card.

Start in the $5-$10 games. They'll be tighter games than the bigger ones because of the ante structure. And the players in this game can't play bigger games because they're not good enough, or they're rocks content to grind out a living in the $5-$10 game. Adjust your play and go after them. If you can't beat this game, don't go on. Play till you can be a steady winner, and then move to $10-$20. Step by step.

Play a number of sessions at each level. You can have a couple of bad streaks or a run of good luck, but in the end, count your money. If you're ahead, move up. If not, stay where you are till you start winning that green.

Or you might then switch to another game. Let's say you can't adjust to 7-Stud, but you're right at home in Hold 'em. Then play Hold 'em. Start with the $3-$6 if there's one, or the $4-$8. Lower games will find eight players seeing the flop. What the hell, they say, it's only a $2 bet to see three cards. It's hard to make moves against smaller players.

Therefore, my best advice is this - if you play in the California or other clubs or in Vegas casinos, then play the game you're best at, that you think you've mastered and can win at. Stick to it. Don't jump to another game just because you need some action. Forget about action. That's not why you're playing poker; that's why the losers are playing poker.

If you find your game is unavailable, let'say a $5-$10 Hold 'em game, take it easy. Relax. If there's an hour's wait for the $5-$10 Hold 'em game, and you've been beating it and are comfortable there, don't jump to a bigger game just because a seat is open. Or play in a smaller game where you'll wind up losing because the stakes bore you and you know you're just killing time. You'll end up losing money.

Even if you find the game you really like at the right stakes, but instead of some loose players there are a bunch of silent rocks waiting for you, get out fast. You'll end up steaming about the rocks, and you don't want to go on tilt in any poker game. Save your money and your temper and take a walk.

Try to get in your favorite game with at least a few weakies in there to beat. I know pros who won't play in a game filled with other locals in Vegas. Then it's just grindtime. They look to find a few tourists and a weak player or two as well. Otherwise they give no action. They take a walk and patiently wait for the right spot. There are a couple of great players who will play in any game at any stake, against anyone, but until you reach that exalted status, pick your spots.

A final word. Play sanely. Don't play with money you can't afford to lose. Don't play if it emotionally devastates you to lose. But the more you know, the better you're going to feel at the table, and if you play a sharp game and remain alert and make the moves we've suggested, the money is going to come your way.

# GLOSSARY

**Ace-high**: Any hand in which the top card is an Ace, such as an Ace-high flush.

**Ante**: Money or chips put into the pot before the deal.

**Babies**: Small cards, usually those with values less than 6.

**Backdoor**: Making a hand that you didn't play for. You play for a full house and make a flush, for example.

**Bad Beat**: A loss when holding a hand that a player was sure would win the pot.

**Bicycle**: Also knows as **Wheel**. A 5-4-3-2-Ace holding in a low hand.

**Big Blind**: The last blind bet, the highest of the blind bets.

**Blank**: A useless card dealt to a hand.

**Blind**: A player who must make an opening bet prior to the deal, no matter what the value of his hand.

**Bluff**: An attempt to force other players out by betting heavily thus representing an inferior hand as the best hand.

**Board**: The cards seen by all the players, either community cards or cards in a player's hand in a game like stud poker.

**Book a Winner (Loser)**: The poker pro's term for his result after a session of play.

**Bring it in**: Also known as **Opening**. The card that must force the action on the first round of betting.

**Bug**: Also known as a **Joker**. A wild card, sometimes with limited value.

**Burn a Card**: The removal of a card from the top of the stock prior to a round of play, put aside out of play by the dealer.

**Button**: A disc used to determine which player is the theoretical dealer in a game such as Hold 'em.

**Buy**: Also **Draw a Card**. The receiving of a card by a player from the stock.

**Call**: Making a bet equal to the previous bet.

**Calling Station**: A player who always calls and rarely raises a previous bet.

**Capping a Raise**: The final, third raise as allowed in most games.

**Cards Speak**: The cards shown by the player to have their best value as seen by the dealer, regardless of the player's call as to the value of his hand.

**Check**: Also **Pass**. Passing one's turn to bet.

**Check and Raise**: A move wherein a player may raise after first checking his hand.

**Cold Call**: Calling a bet and raise at the same time after first checking, or betting for the first time.

**Crying Call**: A weak call, made reluctantly.

**Declare**: A player announcing by use of chips whether he is going high, low or high-low.

**Dead Man's Hand**: The holding of Aces over Eights, the same hand Wild Bill Hickok held when he was shot in the back.

**Dead Money**: Money or chips already bet by a player who now folds his hand.

**Dog**: Also **Underdog**. A player who is a favorite to lose.

**Door Card**: In Stud Poker, the first card open on the initial round of play.

**Draw**: See **Buy**.

**Drawing Dead**: Drawing for a card that will still lose the pot for the player.

**Fast Play**: Betting and raising aggressively.

**Flop**: The first three cards dealt at once in a game like Hold 'em.

**Fold**: To give up the cards and remove oneself from the play of the hand.

**Free Card**: Not having to pay for a card on any round of play.

**Garbage Hand**: A hand of useless junk, not worth playing.

**Gutshot Draw**: Drawing to an inside straight, such as 7-6-5-3. Going for the 4 is a gutshot draw.

**High Hand**: The best hand in any round of poker.

**High-Low Poker**: A game in which the pot is split among the best high and low hands.

**Hole Card(s)**: The card or cards in Stud Poker unseen by the other players.

**Ignorant End of a Straight**: The low end of a Straight, losing to the high end in a game like Hold 'em.

**Inside Straight**: See **Gutshot Draw**.

**Joker**: See Bug.

**Kicker**: An odd card in a draw hand, usually a high card retained for the draw.

**Limp In**: To just call a bet, usually on the first round.

**Live Blind**: A blind who can raise when it is his turn to bet again on the first round of betting.

**Loball**: A variation of poker where the low hand wins.

**Low Hand**: The best low hand on any round of play.

**Monster**: A very powerful hand.

**Muck, Muck Pile**: The cards already discarded by the players during previous rounds of play.

**Nuts**: The absolute best hand in the game, the one that can't lose.

**Offsuit**: A non-matching card of a different suit.

**On Tilt**: To get angry or to let emotions dictate your play at a poker table.

**Open**: Open the Betting: See **Bring it In**.

**Outs**: Having other possible hands develop from the cards held by the player.

**Overcard**: A card on board higher than your pair.

**Paint**: A face card; the Jack, Queen or King.

**Pass**: See **Check**.

**Pat Hand**: A holding of five cards in draw poker that need no drawn card to improve.

**Pay Off, Paid Off**: Forcing a player to call your bet at the river when you have the superior hand.

**Pocket Cards**: The cards dealt face down to players in games like Hold 'em and Omaha.

**Position**: The place of the player at the table in terms of acting on his hand.

**Pot**: The total money or chips on the table after all the betting rounds are over.

**Rag**: A useless card that doesn't improve the poker hand.

**Rake**: The percentage of the pot taken away by the casino or club.

**Rap Pat**: To stand pat in draw poker and not draw any cards.

**River, The River**: The last card dealt to players in games like Hold 'em and Stud Poker.

**Rock**: A player who's ultra tight and will only stay in with best cards.

**Rolled Up**: The first cards dealt in a stud game all of the same rank.

**Rough**: Designating a low hand with several or one card close to the highest card of the low, for example: 8-6-5-4-2.

**Round of Play**: See **Streets.**

**Scare Cards**: Board cards that look to be the best hand.

**Scared Money**: Undercapitalized stakes in a game of poker.

**Scoop, Scoop the Pot**: To take both high and low in a game of High-Low.

**Set**: See **Trips**.

**Setup**: Two new decks of cards put inot play in the club games.

**Showdown**: The showing of cards after the last bets have been made.

**Sidecard**: The other card in the pocket or hole in addition to the best card or cards.

**Slow Play**: Not raising but merely calling or checking.

**Small Blind**: The early blind betting the smallest amount of the blinds.

**Smooth**: A low hand whose other four cards are very low. Such as 8-4-3-2-Ace.

**Spit Card**: An extra card that can be used by all players to form their best hands.

**Stand Pat**: See Rap Pat.

**Steal The Ante**: Raising on the first round of betting in order to drive all the other players out, and then winning the pot, which consists mostly of the antes.

**Steaming**: Getting angry at the table and playing badly.

**Stock**: The cards that have not yet been dealt out.

**Streets**: A term to designate the rounds of betting according to how many cards have been dealt out.

**Table Stakes**: The player is limited to betting only money or chips he or she has on the table.

**Tells**: Gestures or words by a player that give away the value of his hand.

**Trash Hand**: See **Garbage Hand**.

**Trips**: A Three-of-a-kind holding. Sometimes called a **Set**.

**Turn, On the Turn**: Fourth Street in 7-Card Stud and Texas Hold 'em.

**Unconscious Cards** - Winning hands dealt to a player no matter the value of his starting cards.

**Underdog**: See Dog.

**Under the Gun**: The player who must act first in any round of poker.

**Up in the Air**: Designating a pair that is formed on the board. Example: *He has 7s up in the air.*

**Wheel**: See **Bicycle**.

**Wild Card**: A card that can be of any value or rank the player wishes it to be.

# WIN MONEY AT VIDEO POKER! WITH THE ODDS!

## GRI'S PROFESSIONAL VIDEO POKER STRATEGY

**At last,** for the **first time,** and for **serious players only,** the GRI **Professional Video Poker** strategy is released so you too can play to win! **You read it right** - this strategy gives you the **mathematical advantage** over the casino and what's more, it's **easy to learn!**

**PROFESSIONAL STRATEGY SHOWS YOU HOW TO WIN WITH THE ODDS -** This **powerhouse strategy,** played for **big profits** by an **exclusive** circle of **professionals,** people who make their living at the machines, is now made available to you! You too can win - with the odds - and this **winning strategy** shows you how!

**HOW TO PLAY FOR A PROFIT -** You'll learn the **key factors** to play on a **pro level:** which machines will turn you a profit, break-even and win rates, hands per hour and average win per hour charts, time value, team play and more! You'll also learn big play strategy, alternate jackpot play, high and low jackpot play and key strategies to follow.

**WINNING STRATEGIES FOR ALL MACHINES -** This **comprehensive, advanced pro package** not only shows you how to win money at the 8-5 progressives, but also, the **winning strategies** for 10s or better, deuces wild, joker's wild, flat-top, progressive and special options features.

**BE A WINNER IN JUST ONE DAY - In just one day,** after learning our strategy, you will have the skills to **consistently win money** at video poker - with the odds. The strategies are easy to use under practical casino conditions.

**FREE BONUS - PROFESSIONAL PROFIT EXPECTANCY FORMULA ($15 VALUE) -** For serious players, we're including this free bonus essay which explains the professional profit expectancy principles of video poker and how to relate them to real dollars and cents in your game.

To order send just $50 by check or money order to:
Cardoza Publishing, P.O. Box 1500, Cooper Station, New York, NY 10276